Extravaganza One Act Fest
2025

A Collection of Original

One-Act Plays

Published by Idle Hour Press
Compiled by Niki J. Borger
Foreword by Wolfgang Bodison
Cover design by Wolfgang Bodison

Print ISBN: 979-8-9956888-4-6
eBook ISBN: 979-8-9956888-5-3

Library of Congress Control Number: 2026909944

North Hollywood, CA

First Edition 2026

For performance rights or inquiries, please contact the individual authors directly.

"You can wait for permission...

or you can do the work.

That's the choice."

Foreword from the Director

Most people talk about doing the work. Very few actually do it. This festival exists to separate those two things.

The 2025 Extravaganza One-Act Festival is not built on theory, intention, or endless discussion. It's built on action. On artists walking into a room with nothing but an idea—and staying in it long enough, honestly enough, to turn that idea into something alive. No templates. No safety. No imitation. Just point of view.

Every piece started the same way: someone decided to stop waiting. To stop asking for permission. To stop circling the idea of being an artist—and actually become one in practice. That's where this work comes from. And make no mistake—this is work.

It's uncomfortable. It's exposing. It demanded that they confronted what they really thought, what they really felt, and whether they were willing to stand behind it in front of other people. There's no hiding in that. Either something real is happening… or it isn't.

That's what makes this a laboratory. And that's what connects it to the spirit of TesserAct Theater Company—a space where artists don't wait for opportunity, they generate it. Where the goal isn't to look like an artist…

…it's to be one.

Wolfgang Bodison

Table of Contents

ROMEO AND JULIET (ABRIDGED)

by Patrick Kevin

Overview
a 20-minute comedy
for 5 actors, at least 1 male

Synopsis
A staged, abridged production of William Shakespeare's *Romeo and Juliet* is interrupted by a former cast member.

Characters
STAGE MANAGER
JULIET
ROMEO
LEAD   – former Romeo
GHOST   – male, father of *Lead*

Setting
Takes place here and now, on the present stage.

Notes
This is meant to be scrapy and lo-fi, in a black box type setting, with simple props and *Stage Manager* describing luxurious sets and costumes that are not there. Production materials are noted when they should be utilized. *Lead* should act drunk and have an over-the-top, bad, British accent, to emphasize their misguided assumption that good, Shakespearean actors are inherently British, and vice versa. Pronouns and

names can be changed to fit whomever is casted for each role, except for *Ghost*.

Original Premiere

Romeo and Juliet (Abridged) premiered on May 31st, 2025, at the 2025 Extravaganza One Act Fest, directed by Wolfgang Bodison.

Original Cast

STAGE MANAGER – Thanh Tran
JULIET   – Kyle Tran
ROMEO   – Abraham Arias
LEAD   – Patrick Kevin
GHOST   – Henry Foster Brown

Performance Rights

This play may not be performed, reproduced, or adapted without written permission from the author. To request performance rights, please contact Patrick Kevin via patrickfkevin@gmail.com

Scene 1

Lights up. On stage is a STEP-STOOL down stage left, a MUSIC STAND with an open BINDER with the SCRIPT down stage right with a TABLE next to it. On said table is a LARGE, FULL PLASTIC BAG and 2 BASEBALL CAPS: one cap has "NURSE" written on an INDEX CARD that is BINDER CLIPPED onto the back of it and the other cap has "FRIAR LAWRENCE" in the same fashion. A turned around COUCH rests top stage center in between 2 DOORS to backstage. A FOG MACHINE is backstage, out of sight.

STAGE MANAGER, in SHOW BLACKS, stands behind the music stand. They are wearing a WATCH and a FANNY PACK, with 2 attached FRYING PANS and containing a RATCHET STRAP, a KNIFE, and a FLASHLIGHT.

JULIET, in SHOW BLACKS, stands upon the step-stool, wearing a WIG over top a WIG CAP, with a PLASTIC RING in their pocket.

ROMEO, in SHOW BLACKS with a BLACK OVERSHIRT, leans down stage against the couch. They have a FANCY LIQUID CONTAINER WITH A SCREW-ON LID in their back pocket.

A DRAMATIC LOVE THEME begins playing as accent lights come up, starting on Juliet, then Romeo, and finally Stage Manager.

The MUSIC fades down but not out and continues along with the lights going to these dramatic "show lights" whenever the "Romeo and Juliet" show is proceeding.

STAGE MANAGER. *(to Audience)* Thank you all for coming to our abridged production of *Romeo and Juliet*. We hope you enjoy it.

Stage Manager looks down at the script and reads.

STAGE MANAGER. *(reading)* Curtains rise. Act 2, Scene 2. It is a beautiful night outside the Capulet home. Juliet, in a luxurious, hand-sewn gown with exquisitely done hair, stands upon her balcony, calling out into the vast distance of the estate. The evening quiet is broken by the soft hum of the nightlife.

Stage Manager EMOTES various nightlife (frogs, crickets, owls, etc.) including saying things like, "CRICKET" for sound effects.

JULIET. *(not noticing Romeo)* O Romeo, Romeo!
Wherefore art thou Romeo?
Deny thy father and refuse thy name;
Or, if thou wilt not, be but sworn my love,
And I'll no longer be a Capulet.
STAGE MANAGER. *(reading)* Romeo appears from behind the well-curated bushes of the voluptuous Capulet garden.
ROMEO. Shall I hear more, or shall I speak at this?
JULIET. But thy name that is my enemy:

What is Montague? It is nor hand, nor foot-

Stage Manager SNAPS and spins their finger in a circle to get Juliet to speed up. Juliet notices this, reacts, and turns further away from Romeo.

JULIET. -OH, be some other name.
STAGE MANAGER. *(reading)* Romeo rises and makes his way through the exquisite short-hedge maze, closer to Juliet.

Romeo tiptoes down stage center, working through the imaginary bushes, including separating two bushes with his arms and stepping through the newly formed hole. Stage Manager CRINKLES the plastic bag as Romeo moves.
Romeo lands along the same plane as Juliet and Stage Manager, parallel to house.

ROMEO. I take thee at thy word.

Juliet looks down and notices Romeo.

STAGE MANAGER. *(reading)* Romeo ascends the great wall, up to Juliet's balcony, hoisting himself over the banister.

Stage Manager throws out the ratchet strap stage left, in front of Romeo, toward Juliet. After multiple throw attempts, Juliet grabs the other end of the ratchet strap.

ROMEO. *(to Stage Manager)* Hold it tight. Hold it
    tight!

> *Romeo grabs onto and zip-lines up and down
> the ratchet strap multiple times to Juliet, both
> of them reaching out their hands as they get
> closer and then putting them down as they drift
> further apart. As they do this, Stage Manager
> adds in BUZZING sounds that go up and down
> in pitch as Romeo goes up and down for each
> attempt.*
> *Eventually, the two meet. Juliet drops their end
> of the ratchet strap and steps stage right from
> the step-stool and faces Romeo.*
> *Stage Manager pulls back the ratchet strap.*
> *Romeo and Juliet lock into an embrace.*

ROMEO. *(to Juliet)* Call me but love, and I'll be new
    baptized;
    Henceforth I never will be… Montague.
LEAD. *(from up house center)* ROMEO!

> *MUSIC cuts off; lights go to plain, colorless
> "rehearsal lights" during this and any further
> interruptions by Lead.*
> *Romeo breaks character during Lead's
> interruptions. Juliet remains in character
> throughout the entire show. Stage Manager
> does not break their attitude and maintains a
> smile throughout the entire show.*
> *Romeo lets go of Juliet and looks up into house
> to see the source of the outburst. Juliet doesn't
> look away from Romeo and remains in their
> embraced position.*

LEAD, in VERY COLORFUL AND CASUAL ATTAIRE, including a HAWAIIAN OVERSHIRT loosely overtop their T-SHIRT, stumbles down house center, carrying an OPEN BEER CAN.

ROMEO. *(to Lead)* Jesus Christ.
LEAD. *(to Romeo)* Nope, not quite Jesus, just me. And the line is, "I never will be ROMEO!" It's "Romeo," not, "Montague," but an *understudy* wouldn't've known that, ya fuckin' idiot. Only the *true* Romeo, like myself, would've known… would've… not fucked that up.

Lead lands down stage center, diverts up stage right, past Romeo, finishes their beer, crumples it up, and throws it off to the up stage right corner.
Lead turns to face the Audience, coming down stage center, in-between Romeo and Juliet, revealing CHUNKY VOMIT covering the front of their t-shirt.

ROMEO. Dude, Rob, what are you DOING here? *(to Stage Manager)* I thought he was kicked out?

Stage Manager doesn't respond.
Lead locks into Romeo's former position, in Juliet's embrace.

JULIET. *(to Lead)* Art thou not Romeo, and a Montague?

Romeo separates Lead and Juliet, disgusted by getting close to Lead's vomit-covered t-shirt.

ROMEO. *(to Lead)* Are you drunk, again?
LEAD. That's besides the point. I am here to make amends with you all because I've been kinda… I'll *admit*, of a dick.

Lead diverts up stage left, behind Juliet, stumbles down stage and onto the step-stool.

LEAD. *(to everyone)* Great, now that *that's* done with, more importantly, I'm here to honor the legacy of my *late father* by putting on *our* show as the always intended, rightful Romeo! As what once was… oh god, was the case… and shall always be-

Lead steps down from the step-stool and inches down stage and dry-heaves toward an Audience member with the "be" line.

LEAD. *(to Audience member)* Excuse me.

Romeo goes to and drags Lead as dead baby weight toward the up stage right door.

ROMEO. *(while dragging)* "*Our* show?" Rob, you lost that position, fair and square. The director let you go, she was tired of… no, we *all* were tired of you getting drunk every other rehearsal.
LEAD. *(to everyone; while being dragged)* I'm sorry everyone. I was… 've been an asshole, but this is the new me. Trust me, I'm better now, new

and im-improffed. And I, uh… I'm ready to do the show now, so let's uh, let's do the show. C'mon.

Romeo opens the door and shoves Lead through it. Lead pushes against the door, they struggle, but Romeo eventually closes it. Romeo gets back into position on Juliet' right.

STAGE MANAGER. *(to Romeo)* Dude, we gotta go- *(reading)* -Act 3, Scene 2!

MUSIC continues; lights go back to show lights.
Juliet steps back onto the step-stool.

JULIET. *(to Romeo)* Gallop apace you fiery-footed steeds.
ROMEO. *(to Juliet)* It best agrees with night. Come, civil night.

Lead bursts out through the up stage right door. MUSIC stops; lights go to rehearsal lights. Lead heads down stage center.

LEAD. *(to Romeo)* I've already heard this negativity from all of you: from the director, from my sponsor, from the guy at the liquor store, and from… dad, my dad, Pa–
ROMEO. *(to Lead)* Holy shit, here come the water works again: 'Pa' this, 'Pa' that–

Lead comes up on Romeo's right.

LEAD. Hey, you shut the fuck up about him! It's a
    sensitive subject!
ROMEO. Rob, move the fuck on!
STAGE MANAGER. *(reading)* Nurse drops the rope
    ladder.

Juliet looks up.

LEAD. I am moving on!

*Lead moves behind Romeo, up stage left, then
to Romeo's left side, in-between Romeo and
Juliet.*

STAGE MANAGER. *(reading)* Falling, falling….

Lead pushes against Romeo.

LEAD. This is just part of the-

*Lead shoves Romeo onto the ground, stage
right.*

LEAD. -process.
STAGE MANAGER. *(reading)* Thud!

*Juliet watches an invisible rope ladder fall and
land on the ground in front of them.*

LEAD. A long process but still, a process.
JULIET. And Tybalt's death, that would have slain my
    husband.
ROMEO. What process? This whole "moving on,"
    must be going well for you since you've

probably been in this *(indicates Lead's drunkenness)* 'state,' for years.

LEAD. I don't need to take this crap from you, you don't *know* me.

ROMEO. What I do *know* is that you're a spoiled brat who was finally *banned* from this show and this theater when you once again-

Romeo stands back up as Lead turns away and faces Juliet.
Romeo pushes Lead into Juliet, and Juliet then pushes Lead back to Romeo. They do this a couple times.

ROMEO. *(while pushing)* -graced us with your drunken presence, but *then* presented a new layer to your *performance* by proceeding to vomit in-

Romeo grabs Lead and pulls them down stage right in front of an occupied seat as Lead resists.

ROMEO. *(while pulling)* -that seat.
STAGE MANAGER. *(reading)* Nurse–

Stage Manager looks up, attempts to get Romeo's attention and fails.

LEAD. What seat?

Romeo points to the occupied seat.

ROMEO. That seat!

Stage Manager turns their focus to Juliet and indicates for them to take over.
Stage Manager throws Juliet the cap marked "Nurse." Juliet puts on the cap.

STAGE MANAGER. *(reading)* "Nurse" weeps and wails over Tybalt's corpse.

Juliet weeps and wails over Tybalt's corpse.
Lead points to the occupied seat.

LEAD. You're saying *that* I puked in *that* seat right where *that* person is sitting? Sitting in dried vomit?

Juliet takes off the "Nurse" cap and throws it back to Stage Manager.
Juliet pulls out the plastic ring and puts it on.

ROMEO. Yes!
JULIET. *(trying to get attention)* GIVE THIS RING TO MY TRUE KNIGHT!
LEAD. I don't believe you.
ROMEO. We *all* saw it!

Romeo throws Lead to the ground, up stage center.

LEAD. It must have been someone else.

Romeo grabs Lead by the legs and drags Lead to the up stage right door.

LEAD. *(while being dragged)* I'm telling you what I
     told the director: my vomit comes out *yellow*
     because of bile, THAT vomit was *red* because
     of blood, so it *clearly* was someone else.

     *Romeo opens the door, drags Lead through the
     door way, closes and locks the door, and rattles
     the door handle to make sure it's locked.*

ROMEO. *(through door)* Dealing with you is
     impossible!

     Romeo gets back into position next to Juliet.

STAGE MANAGER. *(reading)* Act 4, Scene 1.

     *MUSIC continues; lights go back to show
     lights.
     Juliet puts the ring back in their pocket. Stage
     Manager stares at Romeo.*

STAGE MANAGER. *(to Romeo)* Friar Lawrence-

     *Stage Manager throws Romeo the cap marked
     "Friar Lawrence."
     Romeo puts on the cap and pulls out the fancy
     liquid container with screw-on lid.*

STAGE MANAGER. *(reading)* -provides Juliet with a
     precious vial that will make her appear like
     death.

     Romeo hands Juliet the container.

ROMEO. *(to Juliet; as Friar Lawrence)* O Juliet, I
      already know thy grief
      It strains me past the compass of my wits.

      *During this, Lead struggles to open the up
      stage left door but busts it open, carrying a
      CROWBAR.
      MUSIC stops; lights go to rehearsal lights.
      Lead drops the crowbar, letting it CLANG on
      the ground. Lead slowly weaves around down
      stage right, landing on Romeo's right.*

LEAD. Listen, Stevie, that's what I'm trying to tell
      you: you could be out there in the world, in all
      sorts of *other* shows, *not* dealing with me.
      You're a great actor, very talented, you should
      be the lead in your *own* show!
ROMEO. *(to Lead)* I am the lead! In *this* one!
JULIET. *(to Romeo)* That may be sir, when I may be a
      wife.

      *Lead puts their right hand on Romeo's left
      check and turns them to face them.*

LEAD. *(skeptical)* Are you?

      *Lead spins Romeo down, in front of them, stage
      right.*

ROMEO. *(confused)* Yes.
JULIET. What must be, shall be.

Juliet holds up the container. Lead grabs the cap off of Romeo's head and puts it on their own head.

LEAD. Check this shit out.
JULIET. *(to container)* Give me, give me! O, tell not me of fear!

Lead leans over, rubs Juliet's back, and plays with their hair.

LEAD. *(to Juliet; as Friar Lawrence)* Hold, get you gone. Be strong and prosperous.
ROMEO. No! Those are my lines now!
LEAD. *(to Audience; off of Juliet)* Steven, *he's* clearly much calmer and much happier with me as Romeo. *Everyone* is.

Romeo moves toward Stage Manager. Juliet pretends to drink from the container.

ROMEO. *(to Stage Manager)* This exact disrespect for people and equipment is why he got fired! Am I the only one who cares about this?
STAGE MANAGER. *(to Romeo)* Yep.

Lead slowly approaches Romeo.

LEAD. *(to Romeo)* Of course you're not the only one who cares. I care too. I just… care a lot more than you do. Let me help you.

Lead approaches Romeo's side as Romeo ebbs further down stage right. Lead puts his arm over Romeo's shoulder.

ROMEO. *(to Lead)* Stop it! I don't need your help anymore!

JULIET. Love give me strength. God knows when we shall meet, again.

Juliet slowly, dramatically, and LOUDLY dies. As Juliet dies, they close up the step-stool, and then fall up stage center onto the couch, disappearing from Audience view, apart from their feet.
Stage Manager runs over to grab the step-stool and brings it back to their prop station.

LEAD. *(teasing; while Juliet and Stage Manager perform their actions)* Yes you do. You're my understudy. C'mon, I've already bestowed upon you some of my vast knowledge, but there's plenty more where that came from. Trust me, it'll make you that much better.

Lead leans in closer to Romeo.

LEAD. And hey, maybe, MAYBE, even better than me.

Romeo pushes Lead up stage center.

ROMEO. And there you go, hyping yourself up again to be the best thing since sliced bread! I've heard this story too many times. I did not learn *anything* from you. I only learned what NOT to do.

LEAD. *(turning to anger)* "Learned what not to do?"

ROMEO. Yep.

LEAD. Are you fucking kidding me?

ROMEO. Nope.

LEAD. EVERYTHING you've *learned* about acting, you've learned from me! I spoon fed you ART!

Lead takes off the cap and throws it down on the ground on "ART!"

STAGE MANAGER. *(reading)* A clash of thunder and lightning marks Juliet's demise!

Stage Manager flashes the flashlight and BANGS the pans together multiple times as Juliet adds another WAIL of death.
Stage Manager retrieves the thrown cap.

ROMEO. Are *YOU* fucking kidding me?

LEAD. Nope.

ROMEO. "Spoon fed me art?"

LEAD. Yep.

As Romeo begins this monologue, Lead slowly eats a chunk of vomit off of their shirt. Romeo reacts to this and then slowly stalks Lead in a counter-clockwise circle until going up stage center, toward the couch.

ROMEO. You think you've been giving me helpful advice? Your 'guidance?' Here's some of your wisdom: "method acting is the only way to go, the rest of that shit is for pussies." I almost got my dick bitten off by a rattlesnake after sleeping outside, naked, in the desert because of method acting. Oh, and "make sure to bottle up your deep, emotional traumas, and then let out all of those unresolved feelings on-stage." And finally, "NEVER RELAX!"

Romeo pushes Lead onto the couch, landing on top of Juliet. Juliet MOANS.

LEAD. *(yelling back in agreement)* You shouldn't!

Lead struggles to get back up, stumbling off the couch and falling down onto the ground, while Romeo continues.

ROMEO. What I *did* learn from you is to hate *you*, just like you hate yourself. It's shitty spoiled people like you who are entitled and think they're owed everything on a silver platter.
LEAD. *(hurt)* No, I don't.
ROMEO. You, you DO. You bitched about your name being too small on the poster–
LEAD. It *was* too small. I've earned that!
ROMEO. No, you haven't! *(continuing rant)* You demand a seltzer every five seconds–
LEAD. *(realizing)* Oh, that's what I'm missing.

Lead stands up.

ROMEO. And you refuse to learn any of your lines!
LEAD. That is objectively not true! I remembered that "Romeo" line!

Romeo exaggeratedly CLAPS at Lead and then out to the Audience.

ROMEO. *(sarcastic)* Oh, great! Con-fucking-grats. One line. Jeez, let's roll out the red fuckin' carpet.
(to Audience) Let's roll out the red carpet for this guy!

Lead joins Romeo in the clapping.

LEAD. *(to Audience)* Yeah!
ROMEO. *(to Lead)* Yeah!
LEAD. *(to Romeo)* Yeah! See, you aren't such a self-centered piece of shit after all.

Romeo grabs Lead by the shoulders and attempts to throw them down stage center to the ground.

ROMEO. Shut up! You think you're-

Romeo begins this line and attempts to throw Lead twice before giving up out of weakness.

ROMEO. C'mon, help me.
LEAD. Okay.

Romeo throws Lead down stage center. Lead crawls stage left to the wall while Romeo stalks them, landing down stage center.

ROMEO. You think you're this exquisite wealth of knowledge? You're sad, you're angry, you hate

life, so you hide from it with alcohol! You think your name is your 'unique character trait,' it's what makes you special, worthy? You're not! Unlike you, I have EARNED this position, and I'm tired of you interrupting MY show!

Lead stands up and braces against the stage left wall.

LEAD. *(pleading)* But Steve, please, I *need* to do this show. I *promised* I would do it for Pa.
ROMEO. Why the fuck do you keep bringing up you dad? It's weird.

Lead approaches Romeo stage center.

LEAD. It's none of your fucking business!
ROMEO. Oh really? None of my fucking business?
LEAD. Nope.
ROMEO. You wanna go?

Lead struggles but manages to take off their overshirt and flings it to the ground. Romeo does the same, without the struggle.

LEAD. Yep.

Both Lead and Romeo position themselves, ready to throw punches. They pause for a moment, and then begin weak-slapping each other.
This goes on for a few moments, GRUNTING and EMOTING along the way. They then break to their separate sides of the stage, parallel

*with house. Romeo leans near Stage Manager
with Stage Manager pushing Romeo away
while maintaining a smile.*

ROMEO. *(exhausted)* You ready again?
LEAD. *(exhausted)* Yeah.

> *Both go back to weak-slapping each other for a
> few more moments before breaking apart again.*

ROMEO. *(exhausted)* Rob! Why?!
LEAD. *(exhausted)* Because! Because he's all I *had*
        left!

> *Romeo thinks for a moment before readjusting
> and going down stage left into a spotlight.*

ROMEO. *(as Ghost)* My hour is almost come, son.
        Pity me not, but lend thy serious hearing.
LEAD. *(confused)* Why are you saying lines from
        Hamlet?

> *Romeo eggs Lead on to participate.*

ROMEO. *(as Ghost)* Lend thy serious hearing!
LEAD. *(reluctant and then begrudgingly)* Ah yes,
        speak. I'm all ears, buckaroo.
ROMEO. *(as Ghost)* I am thy father's spirit!

> *Lights flash, DARK, OMNIOUS MUSIC plays,
> and then the lights go out.
> A spotlight shines on the up stage left door. The
> door opens. Out steps GHOST, wearing a*

*BLACK, HOODED CLOAK, enveloped by a
thick layer of FOG.
Ghost confidently walks down stage center into
another spotlight, as Romeo and Lead back
away stage left and right, parallel with house.
MUSIC fades out as Ghost pulls down his
hood, revealing crudely done WHITE
MAKEUP on his face.*

GHOST. *(to Audience)* Destined for a certain term to
walk the night.

Lead completely drops their fake British accent.

LEAD. *(to Ghost)* Pa? Is that *really* you?
GHOST. *(to Lead)* Yes, son, it is I.
LEAD. But, you're dead.
GHOST. No shit I'm dead. I got conjured up because
you're causing a ruckus. Now what do you
mean you *promised* you'd do this show?
LEAD. I promised I'd do it for you, pop-pop.
GHOST. Why?
LEAD. Because, I lost you before you ever got to see
it, dad.
GHOST. Well-

Ghost looks around.

GHOST. -I don't think this is the show you intended to
do.

*Lead crosses down stage right, in front of
Ghost, landing closely on Ghost's right, while*

Romeo crosses up stage left, behind Ghost, landing on Ghost's left.

LEAD. Of course it's not what I intended to do. I just wanted you to be *proud* of me.
GHOST. Son, I am, always have been, and forever will be proud of you. You don't have to prove yourself to me. The only person you have to prove yourself to, is *you.*

Lead moves closer to hug Ghost.

LEAD. Aw, thanks dad. I love you!

Ghost puts his arm up and stops Lead from hugging him.

GHOST. Don't be such a pussy.

Lead looks away from Ghost and down at their feet in shame.

LEAD. *(disappointed)* Oh, I'm sorry, sir.
GHOST. Don't apologize to me, boy. Apologize to everyone here. Now!

The lights come up in house. Lead looks up at the Audience.

LEAD. *(embarrassed)* Yes, sir. *(to everyone)* I'm sorry everyone for having wasted the past… 18-ish minutes of your time. I'm sorry that I ruined this experience of true theatre *(pronounced, "thea-tre")* for you all.

Romeo exaggeratedly COUGHS.

LEAD. *(to Romeo)* And I'm sorry I called you a "self-centered piece of shit," Steve.
ROMEO. Thank you. *(to Ghost)* Thank you, sir.
GHOST. C'mon, I taught you better than that. Alright, let's let these people finish their show.
LEAD. *(to Ghost)* Okay.

> *The lights go down in house and reset to rehearsal lights. DARK, OMNIOUS MUSIC plays as Lead and Ghost exit through the up stage left door, and then fades out, once they exit.*
> *Silence and stillness for a moment.*
> *Romeo heads down stage center to finish the show.*
> *Stage Manager looks down at their watch.*

ROMEO. *(as Romeo)* Thou detestable maw, thou womb of death–
STAGE MANAGER. *(cutting Romeo off)* Welp, time's up!

> *Stage Manager closes their binder, walks over, and stabs Romeo with the knife.*

STAGE MANAGER. *(while stabbing)* Romeo takes Juliet's dagger, stables himself, and dies. The end!

> *Romeo dies.*
> *Stage Manager exits through the up stage left door.*

Juliet YELLS back to life and springs up from the couch. Juliet looks around at the relatively empty stage.

JULIET. *(confused)* Hello? Is the show over?

End of Play.

Curtain Call happens with all of the actors on stage, but with Romeo still dead on the ground.

NINETY SEVEN BEATS
by Niki J. Borger

Overview
a 15-minute drama
for 5 actors, 1 female and 4 any gender

Synopsis
When Micah's heart is down to its final beats, he
bargains for more time with the woman he loves.

Characters
MICAH   – 30s
ARIEL   – any age
ELLIE   – 30s, female, Micah's wife
DOCTOR   – 30s to 60s
NURSE   – 20s to 60s

Setting
Present day. A hospital room. A single hospital bed in
the center of the room. A heartbeat monitor behind it.
Somewhere to the side, a chair.

Notes
All characters but Ellie can be any gender. The lines
should be adjusted accordingly. "On" can be indicated
as a light coming from above the audience. Scene 3
takes place in complete darkness. Alternatively to
producing the sounds and lines on stage, they can be
prerecorded – though a live performance is preferable.
Once the performance has been staged, any lines

indicating the number of heartbeats left should be corrected to represent the actual number.

Original Premiere

Ninety Seven Beats premiered on June 1st, 2025, at the 2025 Extravaganza One Act Fest, directed by Wolfgang Bodison.

Original Cast

MICAH   – Dylan Marusich
ARIEL   – Niki J. Borger
ELLIE   – Erin Hadfield
DOCTOR   – Megan Corse
NURSE   – Rebecca Tarabocchia

Performance Rights

This play may not be performed, reproduced, or adapted without written permission from the author. To request performance rights, please go to https://nikijborger.com/plays

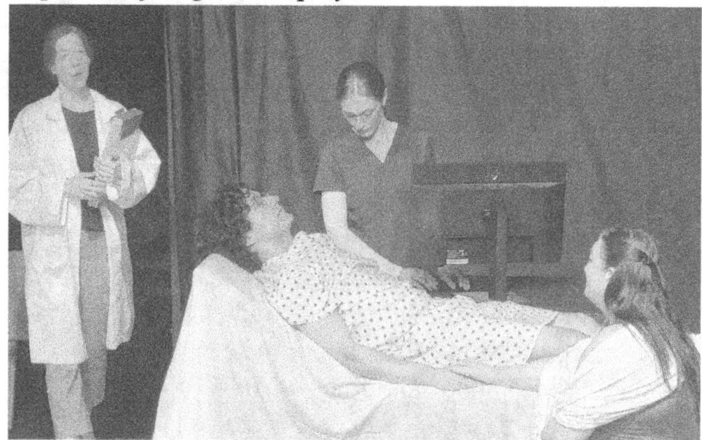

Megan Corse, Dylan Marusich, Rebecca Tarabocchia, Erin Hadfield, photo by Ashley Elsa White

Scene 1

Lights up on a hospital room. A NURSE is pushing a hospital bed into the room. In it is MICAH, motionless. She places a heartbeat monitor by his side and attaches the cables. She draws some blood. The steady beeping of the heart beat monitor can be heard. ELLIE enters in a rush. She checks on Micah, waits, prays. The DOCTOR enters.

DOCTOR. Micah has severe brain swelling. We had to induce a coma.

ELLIE. Wait, you induced a coma without asking me?

DOCTOR. There was no other way. We've run some tests and should have the results by the end of today.

Ellie nods. The doctor leaves. Time passes. Ellie rests her head on Micah's bed. Black.

Scene 2

In the black, the heartbeat sound becomes longer, deeper, and slower, indicating that time has slowed down. Lights up. Ellie's head is still resting on the bed. In the back stands ARIEL.

ARIEL. Micah, wake up.

Micah wakes up with a gasp. Ellie stays motionless.

ARIEL. It's time to go.

Upon moving his hands, Micah realizes that he can, in fact, move. His eyes find Ellie immediately.

MICAH. Hey Ellie.
ARIEL. She's asleep, she won't hear you. Let her rest.

He notices Ariel.

MICAH. Who are you?
ARIEL. You can call me Ariel.
MICAH. You're not a doctor or a nurse, are you? Ellie?
ARIEL. Not quite, no.
MICAH. Then what are you doing here?
ARIEL. I'm here to help.
MICAH. Like a social worker? Ellie?
ARIEL. More like a guardian angel.
MICAH. I have a guardian angel?
ARIEL. No, you don't. *(under her breath)* Not anymore.
MICAH. Then what are you doing here?

A slow, dark heartbeat can be heard.

ARIEL. No more questions. Time to go.
MICAH. Go where?
ARIEL. On.
MICAH. What do you mean, on?
ARIEL. Just on. It's time.
MICAH. You mean, like to heaven?
ARIEL. Well...

MICAH. Am I dying?
ARIEL. Yes, you are, Micah.

Micah wasn't ready for this. No one ever is.

MICAH. No, no, no. That can't be. I'm feeling great!
    I'm not dying. You got the wrong guy.
ARIEL. It's definitely you. Come on, let's go!
MICAH. Then how come I feel amazing? Look, I can
    move everything. I got energy. I got moves. I'm
    thrivin'!
ARIEL. That's what it feels like when you shed a
    human shell.
MICAH. I don't think I've ever felt better before! Just,
    just take someone else.
ARIEL. I can't do that.
MICAH. Like, you don't want to, or you can't?
ARIEL. I can't, it's your turn.
MICAH. What do you want? I promise I'll be good
    from here on. I'll work harder, I'll help
    others… I can go to church! I promise, I'll go
    to church every Sunday, or every day, if you
    want me to.
ARIEL. I'm not here to negotiate.
MICAH. Then go away! I'm not dying today!

A very loud heartbeat interrupts him.

MICAH. What the–
ARIEL. Hear that?
MICAH. Kinda hard to miss.
ARIEL. That's your heart. It has 86 beats left–
MICAH. What?
ARIEL. Then it will stop. And when it does–

MICAH. How do you know that?
ARIEL. When it does, trust me, it will be a lot easier
        for everyone if you've come with me
        voluntarily.
MICAH. Voluntarily? So I do have a choice?
ARIEL. Not on whether–
MICAH. I'm choosing to stay.
ARIEL. Micah–
MICAH. I can't leave.
ARIEL. Why not?
MICAH. Because of my wife.

Micah indicates Ellie.

ARIEL. Ellie.
MICAH. All my life, she's taken care of me.
ARIEL. That was very kind of her–
MICAH. Since we were little kids! We're both
        orphans. Every time I got beaten up, or an
        adoption failed, or I just wanted to give up…
        she's been there for me. I owe her so much, I
        can't just leave her.
ARIEL. I can assure you, Ellie doesn't feel like you
        owe her anything.
MICAH. But she needs my help now! She just lost her
        job–
ARIEL. I know.
MICAH. If I'm gone, what will happen to her?
ARIEL. She'll figure it out.
MICAH. That's all you got? She'll figure it out? If I
        die, she'll be all alone.
ARIEL. She won't be alone.
MICAH. How can you know that?
ARIEL. She's got– *(stops herself)*… friends, right?

MICAH. Yes, she does have some good friends.
ARIEL. There you go.
MICAH. But it's not the same. I want to be the one
        who is there for her. She's my wife!
ARIEL. It is not your choice when you get to enter this
        life or leave it. And when you can't choose it,
        you are not responsible for the consequences.
MICAH. But I want to be. Please, let me be.
ARIEL. There will always be things unfinished. You
        have to trust that others will finish them for
        you.

        *A moment of silence. Only the long, dark, slow
        heartbeat can be heard.*

ARIEL. Time is running short. We need to go.
MICAH. You're just being mean on purpose! I thought
        you were my guardian angel?
ARIEL. I'm not.
MICAH. Are you the devil? Is that what this is about?
        You're trying to make my life hell.
ARIEL. The only hell that exists is the powerlessness
        you choose.
MICAH. You sound like the devil! This is evil!
ARIEL. Stop being so childish. You were given the gift
        of life. It's nothing you've earned or you're
        entitled to. Now, it will be taken away. You
        have no right to complain.
MICAH. What about my future? All the things I didn't
        get to do yet? Aren't they part of the life
        experience?
ARIEL. Like what?
MICAH. Like… I want to grow old! With my wife!
        You know, sitting on a porch, drinking coffee,

eating whatever I want, telling the neighbors off for being too loud or parking the wrong way... And then, my buddy and I, we've been working on this new type of bioplastic. It's so cool! It dissolves when you put it in salt water. We want to make it a business. Reduce plastic waste. Clean up the planet... do our part… And, jeez– what day is it?

ARIEL. It's Friday, Micah.

MICAH. What time?

ARIEL. 6.34–

MICAH. am or–

ARIEL. pm. You fell into a coma earlier this morning.

MICAH. Shit! Ellie and I, we had a doctor's appointment. OBGYN. About having children. We think we're ready. For kids, I mean. We want a boy and a girl, but I'm sure we'll be happy no matter what. Our own family. I can't wait to know what that'll be like.

ARIEL. I get that.

MICAH. What about all these things? If I was given the gift of life, don't I have a right to the full experience?

ARIEL. What exactly is it that you want?

MICAH. What do you mean?

ARIEL. Growing old. Why would you want that?

MICAH. So I know what it feels like!

ARIEL. Haven't you grown older since the day you were born?

MICAH. Yes, but–

ARIEL. Why do you want to build a business?

MICAH. So I can try new things, see what works, and then do it better.

ARIEL. Don't you do that every day of your life? Why
       do you want to have kids?
MICAH. So I know what it's like to love and be loved
       eternally.
ARIEL. But you already do.

They both look at Ellie. Another heartbeat.

ARIEL. Most of what we seek has always been right in
       front of us. But it often takes the imminence of
       loss to recognize it.
MICAH. You're right. Please don't make me leave her.
ARIEL. It's neither your choice nor mine. Come on, let
       us go.
MICAH. But where am I going? You're not taking me
       to hell, are you?
ARIEL. You're only going to be in hell if you don't
       come with me now.
MICAH. But I haven't done anything bad! I haven't
       hurt anyone, I always tried my best to be good–
ARIEL. Yes, you did. We have to–
MICAH. Then please, I have no place in hell, I belong
       in heaven–
ARIEL. That is not my choice to make. Time is
       running–
MICAH. Then whose choice is it? Please, wait. Are
       you quite, quite certain that I'm dying?
ARIEL. Absolutely.
MICAH. And there's nothing that can be done about it?
       No treatment or anything?
ARIEL. Nothing at all.
MICAH. Then can you at least tell me what I'm
       facing? Will there be a test? Do I have to weigh
       my soul?

ARIEL. All I can tell you is not to worry about that,
    Micah, please, let's just go!

The heart beat is speeding up again.

MICAH. How can I not worry about it?
ARIEL. Micah, we're running out of time! I need you
    to come with me!

Ellie starts moving very slowly.

MICAH. Ellie, Ellie, hey, I'm here. Can you hear me?

She doesn't react to him at all.

ARIEL. She can't hear you, Micah. Come on, only
    four beats left.
MICAH. Ellie, please!
ARIEL. Three. You'll end up in hell if you stay now!
MICAH. I'm okay! I'll be fine!
ARIEL. Two. You have to go on, so you can be reborn
    again.
MICAH. Just look at me, please! Ellie!
ARIEL. One. Micah, this is your last chance!

*Ellie awakes with a gasp. The heartbeat
monitor stops beeping. Micah passes out, as all
goes black.*

ELLIE. Micah! MICAH!!! Help! Somebody? Please,
    help!!!

Scene 3

This entire scene takes place in the black. The door bursts open, followed by the Nurse's footsteps entering the room.

NURSE. Code blue! Doctor to 204!

The Doctor comes rushing in, pushing a crash cart.

ELLIE. Micah, don't leave me!
NURSE. BP's dropping, no pulse!
DOCTOR. Starting compressions! Charge to 200 joules.
NURSE. Charging... Clear!

The sound of a defibrillator can be heard.

DOCTOR. Still no rhythm. Charge to 300.
ELLIE. Micah!
DOCTOR. Oxygen stats critical.
NURSE. Charging... Clear!

The sound of the second defibrillator attempt.

DOCTOR. Nothing. One more time. Charge to 360.
NURSE. Charging... Clear!
ELLIE. Come back to me! Please!

The sound of the third defibrillator attempt. Finally, the beeping of the heart beat monitor resumes.

NURSE. We've got rhythm!
DOCTOR. He's back.

*Ellie's heavy breathing eases. Slowly, the crash
cart is pushed out of the room again. Both the
nurse and the doctor leave. The door closes.*

Scene 4

*Lights up. Micah is lying in bed, motionless.
The heartbeat can be heard. Ellie is standing to
one side of Micah's bed, and Ariel is standing
on the other.*

ARIEL. I'm so sorry, Micah. You could've chosen
    your next life, but you chose hell instead.

The doctor enters, addressing Ellie.

DOCTOR. The worst has been confirmed. It's bacterial
    meningitis. Micah will never wake up again.

Ellie breaks into tears.

ARIEL. It wasn't my place to answer your questions.
    See, I'm not your guardian angel, but hers.

*Ariel approaches Ellie and puts one hand on
her shoulder.*

DOCTOR. There is no hope for recovery. Micah left
    you in charge. Sooner or later, you will have to
    make a very hard decision.

ELLIE. I don't understand. You're gonna make me kill
the love of my life?

Black.

End of play.

FREE TRIAL OF FAITH

by Joe Doza and Drue Delio

Overview
a 15-minute drama
for 3 actors, 1 female, 2 male, and 1 male VO

Synopsis
A young Mormon missionary, driven by duty, encounters an unexpected challenge that forces him to confront his most profound beliefs.

Characters
ALEX – Male, late teens/early 20s, A Mormon missionary driven by faith and duty, but naïve.
DAX – Male, late 20s, masking darker intentions.
GINA – Female, mid-20s, practical and empathetic, grounded with everyday life.
NEWS REPORTER – VO

Disclaimer
This is a work of fiction. While it may reference historical events or real individuals, all dialogue and dramatic elements are fictionalized for artistic purposes.

Setting
Scene 1: A cluttered ranch room with peeling wallpaper, a dusty couch, a rickety coffee table, and a vintage guitar.
Scene 2: A modest city apartment in soft morning light.

Notes
Minimal props required. A guitar may be mimed or played live. The news bulletin can be delivered as a recorded sound cue or read live as a voice-over.

Original Premiere
Free Trial of Faith premiered on May 31st, 2025, at the 2025 Extravaganza One Act Fest, directed by Wolfgang Bodison.

Original Cast
ALEX – Joe Doza
DAX   – Drue Delio
GINA – Niki J Borger

Performance Rights
This play may not be performed, reproduced, or adapted without written permission from the author. To request performance rights, please contact drue.delio@gmail.com

Scene 1

A small, cluttered room with peeling wallpaper and a dusty couch sits center stage, next to a rickety coffee table covered in old magazines, a half-empty ashtray, and a vintage guitar leaning against the wall, as the scene begins.

DAX. *(on phone)* Yes, boss, yes. Ohm, absolutely. You can count on me; I'll be there, boss. Will do. Thank You, Johnny.

A sudden knock at the door. Dax pauses, glances toward the door, then continues rolling the joint, unfazed.

The knocking resumes, louder and more insistent. Dax hesitates, then deliberately ignores it, focusing on the task at hand.

The knocking continues, now rhythmic and unyielding. Dax's expression shifts from irritation to curiosity, then to resignation. Set down the joint, rise slowly, and move toward the door.

DAX. Hello?!
ALEX. Hi, I'm Alex
DAX. Yeah…Hey Alex
ALEX. I'm from the Mormon Church of Apostolic United Brethren. Can I talk to you for a few minutes?
DAX. The Mormon church?!
ALEX. Yea!

Dax swings the door open.

DAX. Just don't try to baptize me. Haha, Welcome to Spahn Ranch, Alex. Actually, you know what I'm curious about? How do you guys usually do this? You've got a script or anything? Or is it all just improv?

ALEX. I'm here to talk about... God and well, about finding peace. Real peace. The kind that doesn't come from the world, but from something bigger. Something eternal.

DAX. Peace, huh? No thanks, I've heard enough.

ALEX. Well, not exactly.

DAX. Yeah, well, I'm not sure how much I believe in 'peace', especially when it comes with a pamphlet.

Alex tries to stay calm, nervously shuffling through his materials, unsure of how to proceed.

ALEX. It's about... offering something that really matters. Something that could change lives.

DAX. Oh, trust me, I'm all for 'life changes.' But usually, it's just me cleaning out my closet, getting rid of my old concert T-shirts. Maybe a new girlfriend. Not sure a pamphlet's gonna do the trick.

ALEX. I understand. I get that, and you might not understand now, but this mission has helped me a lot. And I'm just trying to help people find what I've found... You don't have to believe right at this moment, but if you come visit the church–

DAX. This mission of yours feels more like a cult. Do you get paid for this, or is it just a free trial of faith?

ALEX. No, no, it's not like that! This is about love and harmony. It's... It's about the calling.

DAX. Oh, so you're saying this is your calling... You have to do this. It's like a... some sort of sacred duty? Oh, that'd be a cool name for a song, huh! Sacred duty

Dax rushes over to get his guitar. And starts playing guitar.

ALEX. Listen, if I don't bring more people in... I'm finished. The prophet, he's... he's not forgiving. And after what happened last time... they'll send me home. I'll lose everything.

DAX. After last time?

ALEX. Yeah, but it's nothing really.

DAX. No- No, tell me what it is? I insist

ALEX. I really shouldn't.

DAX. You'd better tell me, or I won't stop playing.

ALEX. I just can't do it.

DAX. I just can't hear you.

ALEX. Okay! Seriously?! Whatever! I'll say it…. but this is just between you and me… he's been eyeing my girlfriend... in a way that makes me? You know…. feel like he might want to take her for himself. I'm worried about my girlfriend. Are you going to help me or not?!

Dax, while still playing the guitar. Alex, frustrated, waits a few beats and then turns to leave. Dax slowly stops playing the guitar, now intrigued, and grabs a chair.

DAX. So you want to talk about your girlfriend?

Alex smiles while not really wanting to do it. Looks at the chair and sits down with energy.

ALEX. Okay, yeah, let's do it.

DAX. Yeah, I'd like to, but before I do that, I read somewhere that the Mormon church practices polygamy. Your prophet, he uhm…?

ALEX. *(nervously/funny)* The church doesn't teach polygamy in the way you're thinking. It's more about... family. As for my girlfriend. I'm in love with her and would love to build a life with her, and her only.

DAX. And you think your prophet cares about you? Johnny is family. You're running around hiding behind this mission, thinking you can save everyone else without facing what's going on inside you. And trust me, you're never gonna find what you're looking for in that church. Not for yourself, and definitely not for Polly.

ALEX. Yeah, well, you wouldn't understand and

Alex gets up. Shocked.

ALEX. Wait... I never said her name. All I said was 'my girlfriend.' How do you know her name?!

DAX. Who's Squeaky?

ALEX. No, Polly? My girlfriend...?

DAX. Yeah, she goes by Squeaky now, and she's been helping out here at the ranch for a while now.

You know, horseback riding lessons, feeding the animals, that kind of stuff. She's got a real way with horses. And people, apparently.

ALEX. She never told me any of this.

DAX. Guess she didn't think it was a big deal. Or maybe she just didn't want you to worry. She's been... let's say, 'searching' for something. You know how it is. Seems like people only come here when they're looking for answers. Or running from something.

ALEX. Running from what? Me? Is that what you're saying?

DAX. Hey, man, I'm just the messenger. But yeah, she's talked about you. About how you've been... what's the word? Distant. Preoccupied. Always working, always on this 'mission' of yours. She said it's like you're not even there anymore.

ALEX. That's not true! I've been trying to

DAX. *(interrupting)* Trying to save everyone else, I get it? Except her. Funny how that works.

ALEX. You've been questioning her? How'd you know all this?

DAX. People talk, Alex. And I listen. You'd be surprised what you hear when you're not busy preaching. Plus, Squeaky is not exactly subtle. She's got a lot on her mind, alright? –- I'll tell you what, I got an idea. Look, I'll make you a deal with you. You want me to come to your church? Fine. I'll show up, sit in the pews, maybe even sing along if the hymns are catchy. But in exchange, you come with me this Saturday to my buddy Manor's place on Sunset Dr

ALEX. Manor? As in... Jerry Manor? Sunset Dr? … and why would I want to do that? You think Polly will be there?

DAX. Because it's where everything happens. It's where the 'movers and shakers' are. Ya want to save souls, right? Well, there's no better place to start than with the people who think they don't need saving. And Polly will be there, I'll have her drive us if anything, but she wouldn't miss it for the world.

ALEX. I'm not sure why you'd want me there, but... if this gets me to her... if it helps me keep my mission on track...

DAX. She's part of the scene now. Horses, art, music, religion... It's all connected. You want to fix things with her? This is your chance. But you gotta show up. No excuses.

ALEX. Right. No excuses. Got it. I'll... keep that in mind. I just didn't catch your name.

DAX. All my friends call me Dax, Dax Hudson…

Scene 2

Everything feels still, yet alive, a perfect moment, with the quiet promise of possibility. The stage glows with soft morning light in a modest city apartment. GINA, mid-20s, is doing a TV workout, when she suddenly hears a knock on the door. She opens the door.

GINA. Can I help you?

ALEX. Hi, I'm Alex. I'm from the Apostolic United Brethren Mormon Church. I just wanted to take a few minutes to share a message of hope with you.

GINA. Hope, I could use some hope, sure. Come In.

ALEX. Thank you for letting me in. I'm excited to tell you about the community that I'm a part of. Here at the Church of Apostolic United Brethren, we believe in... well, we believe in the power of family, unity, and finding peace through–

Suddenly, a NEWS REPORTER's voice on the TV catches their attention. Gina raises the volume.

NEWS REPORTER. *(voice-over from TV)* Breaking News! Five victims, including actress Lyra Monroe, were brutally slaughtered overnight at 20040 Sunset Dr, a Beverly Hills estate. Police allege the killings bear the hallmarks of John Lawson's murderous cult. Suspects named: Lawson follower 'Dax' Hudson, along with Lena Corvane and Sarah Owens, who allegedly carried out the attacks. While cult member 'Squeaky" or Polly Kade was not directly linked to this massacre, she certainly has ties to Lawson's extremist circle, underscoring the group's chilling reach.

GINA. *(lowers the volume and addresses Alex)* I could really use that prayer now

ALEX. Never mind...

Alex leaves. Lights fade to black.

End of Play.

IT'S NOT YOU IT'S CALICO!

by Drue Delio

Overview
a 30-minute comedy
for 2 actors, 1 female, 1 male, and 2 male or female VO

Synopsis
In 1970, Vinny, who runs a cat shelter and loves Burt
Bacharach, has trouble moving on after his girlfriend
dies of cancer, especially after he meets a new girl,
Tabby.

Characters
VINNY   – male, 20s to 40
CALICO   – female, 20s to 40, same actor as Tabby
TABBY   – female, 20s to 40, same actor as Calico
CALI GHOST   – female, 20s to 40, same actor as Calico
PIZZA OWNER – male/female, 20 to 99, VO
BUDDHIST NEIGHBOR – male/female, 20 to 99, VO

Setting
Silverlake, CA in 1970.

Notes
Wardrobe, furniture, props to reflect the 1970. Calico
and Tabby are two different characters played by the
same actor. Calico has long straight hair and Tabby has
an Afro, implementing wigs in the production. For the
set, the stage is divided in two sides with a door frame
positioned center stage in the middle and
perpendicular to the audience. On stage right of the

door frame, there is a couch, a coffee table, and a
nightstand for the phone. On stage left, there is a small
table with 2 chairs for the pizza parlor scenes.
The split set is simple in nature. This play was inspired
by Keyanna Burgher's original one act, *"It's Not
You, It's Time."* Thank you very much, Keyanna
Burgher.

Original Premiere
It's Not You It's Calico! premiered on May 31st, 2025,
at the 2025 Extravaganza One Act Fest, directed by
Wolfgang Bodison.

Original Cast
VINNY   – Drue Delio
CALICO   – Lynette Garcia-Arguleta
TABBY   – Lynette Garcia-Arguleta
CALI GHOST   – Lynette Garcia-Arguleta
PIZZA OWNER   – Sonny Schnapf
BUDDHIST NEIGHBOR – Sonny Schnapf

Performance Rights
This play may be performed, reproduced, or adapted
without written permission, if proper
credit is given to the author.

Drue Delio and Lynette Garcia-Arguleta,
photo by Joe Doza

Scene 1

Lights up. VINNY (stage right), on phone with his mom. TABBY (stage left) breaking fourth wall and talking to audience as if she's speaking her diary out loud instead of writing it.

TABBY. I think I'm in love. And he's different. But I don't want to get ahead of myself. I'm tired of meeting losers. And the problem is I don't know they are until later. Like my last boyfriend Michael. He never told me he also had a boyfriend.

VINNY. *(On phone.)* Hey mom. No, I'm not OK! I met someone. No that's bad! She's beautiful and I can't stop thinking about her. No that's bad.

TABBY. Like at the pizza parlor I thought we were having fun, and then he cut it short. When I'm with him I don't think about dating anyone else, but I don't think he feels the same. What if he's a serial killer like Peter? I should ask what she does for a living.

VINNY. She looks just like Cali. Like exactly...it's crazy...except for her hair. Cali had long hair like Janice Joplin. Tabby has an Afro...what...no mom, she's not in the Black Panther Party.

TABBY. Like at the pizza parlor, I thought we were having fun and then he cut short. When I'm with him, I don't think about dating anyone else, but I don't think he feels the same. What if he's a serial killer like Peter? I should ask him what he does for a living.

VINNY. Like at the pizza parlor. That's where I met her. When I first saw her, I had all these old feelings come up. She looked so much like Cali. I felt sick. No, it's not in my head, because I peed my pants!

TABBY. He's funny and sweet in a quirky sort of way. He has a big heart. He always gives his pizza crust to the stray cat outside. I think that's what I like about him the most, his heart. He reminds me of Antonio, except he's not in prison.

VINNY. This new girl looks so much like her it won't work out. I guess I'm just not over Cali. I need more time. I miss her, I miss her smile. Whenever she smiled, she used to tilt her head like a dog. I miss her long hair. It was just like Cher's. She always made me laugh when she did her Cher impressions, she was so funny. And she was a horrible dancer, but she didn't care. She was so committed. She was inspiring. I want to be over her, but I'm not. No, mom, don't send me chicken soup. I love you too. Bye.

Scene 2

Stage right (VINNY'S apartment). Flashback. VINNY and CALI are sleeping on the couch. He wakes up. The stereo is still playing. He sees his bong on the coffee table and tries to grab it without waking her up. He grabs it, takes a hit,

*and then starts coughing. She wakes up
suddenly...*

CALI. What time is it?!?
VINNY. *(Playful.)* How would I know?
CALI. Ohhh!! I'm gonna be late for my chemotherapy!
     Why did you move to Silverlake anyway? I
     gotta go.
VINNY. Wait! I have a surprise for you.
CALI. *(Stops and turns around.)* A surprise?
VINNY. Yes. Pick a hand. *(Has his hands behind his
     back, each holding a ticket.)*
CALI. That one.
CALI. *(He gives one it to her.)* What is it?
VINNY. That? These? Oh, they're only tickets to the
     greatest act in the entire universe!
CALI. You got Zeppelin tickets?!?! *(She hugs him.)*
VINNY. Nooo… Burt Bacharach! … See?
CALI. Oh my gosh that's even better! Wait...its 6
     months away,
     VINNY. I know I can't wait.
CALI. Come on, Vinny. The doctor said I'm lucky I'm
     still alive.
VINNY. *(Brushes it off.)* He always says that, and he'll
     say it again next time you see him. Trust me.
     (They hug.)
CALI. OK well, you hold on to them at least. I'll... lose
     them...Thanks for being with me Vinny and
     taking care of me. I wouldn't be able to go
     through this without you I'm so glad I met you
     I love you Vinny.
VINNY. *(Phone rings.)* Oh, lemme get that! *(Vinny
     picks up phone.)* Oh, hey mom. Hold on. *(To
     Cali.)* I'll call you later Cali bye! *(To mom.)*

Hey mom what's up? Oh no, she's leaving for chemo now. *(Vinny waves goodbye to Cali and turns away while Cali is at doorway.)* CALI. Goodbye Vinny. *(She leaves.)*

VINNY. *(Sees her yellow beanie hat on couch.)* Wait! your hat!! *(To mom on phone.)* Oh, I'll give it to her later.

Scene 3

Godfather pizza parlor (stage left.) VINNY sitting alone at table looking at menu. A server comes up.

TABBY. Do you know what you want? *(Pause.)* Is that a no? *(Pause.)* Are you one of those special people?

VINNY. Oh no... I'm not special. I mean I am but not like that… never mind. I'm sorry you look exactly like someone I know.

TABBY. Hey its cool...who?

VINNY. Oh, it doesn't matter. Hi I'm Vinny. With a 'Y'

TABBY. Hi I'm Tabby.with a 'Y'. But you can call me Moonslice.

VINNY. Moonslice?

TABBY. Yea it means enlightened one of the spirit gods.

VINNY. Cool where did you get that name?

TABBY. Detroit.

VINNY. How tall are you?

TABBY. 5'2…5'5 with my Afro.

VINNY. Just like her…

TABBY. What?

VINNY. Oh, I dunno... ha ha.

TABBY. OK… do you know what you want yet?

VINNY. I do. Can I get a slice of cheese?

TABBY. That's it after all this?

VINNY. Yea.

TABBY. *(She goes to back. He eyes her then he fixes his hair before she comes back out.)* Here's your slice. *(Starts walking away.)*

VINNY. Oh, could I get something else?

TABBY. *(Turns around.)* What?

VINNY. Hot pepper... yeah hot pepper... do you have hot pepper?

TABBY. I'll be back. *(She brings pepper and starts to walk away.)*

VINNY... wait!!

TABBY. Yea?

VINNY. *(Pause. He thinks of something else so he can look at her again.)* Do you have any Parmesan cheese?

TABBY. Sure. *(She leaves and comes back with the cheese. She stands there waiting for him to ask for something else.*

VINNY. Oh, I'm good.

VINNY. *(As she turns to walk away.)* I could use some napkins.

TABBY. Like the ones right in front of you?

VINNY. Oh yeah these are good.

TABBY. Are you OK?

VINNY. Yeah... why do you ask?

TABBY. Cool. *(Starts to walk away.)*

VINNY. It's just that you remind me of someone I know.

TABBY. *(Playing along.)* Well, is she pretty?

VINNY. Yeah, we used to go out. She was the love of
        my life. She's dead now.
TABBY. Umm…
VINNY. I didn't kill her if that's what you're thinking.
TABBY. Umm... I wasn't thinking that.
VINNY. Oh…then never mind. *(Pause.)* This is
        awkward, isn't it?
TABBY. Yep
VINNY. I'm sorry you looked familiar but then I felt
        something else… I'm sorry... *(He notices a
        button she's wearing on her collar.)* I like your
        Burt Bacharach button.
TABBY. Oh thanks.
VINNY. *(Long pause.)* Do you want to go to a Burt
        Bacharach concert with me tomorrow night? I
        have an extra ticket...oh that was stupid…
        never mind.
TABBY. What?
VINNY. Huh?
TABBY. What did you say?
VINNY. I said...will you go to a Burt Bacharach
        concert with me.... then I said... that was
        stupid…never mind. *(Awkward pause.)* Will
        you? Or... no…never mind. I'm sorry…but do
        you? I mean you're wearing a Burt Bacharach
        button.
TABBY. I do love me some Burt Bacharach. But you're
        sort of random man.
VINNY. *(Heartfelt.)* I know, but I'm not random
        dangerous, I'm just random random. I act weird
        when I'm nervous...like now. I just saw you and
        wanted to get to know you. Look I promise I'm
        not crazy or anything. I'll even pick you up here
        after work and we can head out.

TABBY. Hmm...it is a tough ticket to get, nothing weird right?

VINNY. Are you kidding me? Nothing weird is my middle name. *(She's not amused.)* It's really Darryl.

TABBY. *(Laughs.)* OK OK, yeah. What the hell, yeah... Let's go.

VINNY. Cool we're gonna have fun. *(He gets up to leave.)* I'll see *you* here tomorrow. *(He extends his hand. As they shake hands, Vinny starts to feel queasy and hunches over.)* Ohh... Um... I gotta go! See you. I'll call you... bye! *(He runs out.)*

TABBY. Um bye.

Scene 4

An improv scene. (Stage left.) Possibly hippie background music playing. VINNY and TABBY walking outside after the concert. He stops her to show her a magic trick. He does a very weak rendition of the disappearing silver coin trick. She is impressed. Then She proceeds to do a magic trick of her own, a weather type witchcraft ritual...beating her chest... yelling... kissing the ground. It starts to thunder and rain! He can't believe it. As its pouring rain, she performs another quick rain ritual to make it stop raining. Vinny is flabbergasted. They walk out.

Scene 5

*Stage left. Godfather pizza parlor. VINNY and
TABBY are sitting down at a table.*

TABBY. So, this is our 72-hour anniversary!

VINNY. *(Coy.)* Oh yes. So it is.

TABBY. *(She looks around.)* You know I work here,
      right?

VINNY. Yea…is this cool? I thought it'd be romantic
      because this is where we met.

TABBY. You know what? It is. This will give me a
      different perspective on the place.

PIZZA OWNER. *(V.O.)* TABBY. set up table 1!!

TABBY. *(yells back)* I'm not working!

VINNY. Sorry.

PIZZA OWNER. *(V.O.)*. TABBBBBY. set up table 3!!

TABBY. I'm not working!!

VINNY. Sorry.

PIZZA OWNER. *(V.O.)* TABBYYYY. Bathroom
      cleanup!

TABBY. *(To the back.)* I said I'm not at work and if
      you call me again, I will go back there and
      literally murder you and then go to your home
      and literally murder your entire family!! *(To
      Vinny.)* Sorry.

VINNY. No, I'm sorry Tabby.

TABBY. It's OK, you can't help it you're a Capricorn
      and that's why I love you.

VINNY. That stuff is fake.

TABBY. Oh really? Like when I made it rain. Cuz it's
      based on science. When the 8th moon of
      Mercury overshadows Venus's fifth dark moon
      it causes electromagnetic waves of energy and

since the Earth is a magnetic force it's going to compensate by following nature's order of the universe... Don't you get it?

VINNY. *(Pause.)* Yeah, I guess.

TABBY. I got you something!

VINNY. So did I! *(They both take something out.)*

TABBY. You remembered!

VINNY. Yeah Open it.

TABBY. No, you.

VINNY. No, you...

TABBY. *(Starts to get flirty.)* No, you open yours.

VINNY. Nooo...you open yours.

TABBY. OK! *(She opens box and takes out a yellow beanie.)*

VINNY. It's a yellow beanie! You know!? To put it on your head. Put it on!

TABBY. *(Surprised, puts it on.)* Thank you.

VINNY. No flip the lid up.

TABBY. Like this?

VINNY. Yeah...Oh my gosh. It looks perfect.

TABBY. Open yours.

VINNY. OK, OK. *(Vinny opens box, a ring of two keys, he holds them up.)* Oh cool... what are these? Did I lose my keys? These aren't my keys... are these keys to the pizza parlor?!? I can eat here whenever I want!?

TABBY. No! They're the keys to my apartment.

VINNY. Oh...

TABBY. You said you hated your apartment, and your lease is up, and they're gonna raise the rent, and your landlord won't let you keep your lizard. Move in with me!

VINNY. Oh, my stomach...

TABBY. Are you OK? Did you pee your pants?

Scene 6

Stage right. Vinny and Tabby enter her apartment in middle of conversation.

VINNY. You sure?
TABBY. Yea!
VINNY. I don't know... it still felt weird to me.
TABBY. A lot of people make out in movie theaters.
VINNY. During The Aristocats?
TABBY. 'Yes, especially The Aristocats.
TABBY. *(They sit on couch. Tabby is flirty.)* Don't you feel kinda… frisky?
VINNY. You know that movie was kinda hot.
TABBY. *(Singing theme.)* "Everybody wants to be a cat..." *(She moves closer.)*
VINNY. *(Vinny starts to retract and sees small creepy shrine on table.)* What is that?
TABBY. *(Still flirty.)* A ghost portal I made.
VINNY. Does it work?
TABBY. I hope so. I talk to my great great great grandmother with it.
VINNY. Oh... how is she?
TABBY. Well, she doesn't have the black plaque anymore. *(They're close to each other on the couch and start to kiss.)*
VINNY. *(He makes a noise and pulls away.)* I am soooo sorry!
TABBY. Did you just throw up in my mouth?!?
VINNY. *(He nods, tries to hurry out.)* Only a little bit!! Um… here's some gum! Oh, shoot I have to go, I have to open the cat shelter early tomorrow! I love you! Bye!! *(Vinny exits.)*

Scene 7

*Split stage with VINNY. (stage right) on phone
in his apartment, TABBY is stage left.*

VINNY. Hey mom. No, I'm not good! I saw Tabby
again and it's getting serious. No that's bad! On
our anniversary she asked me to move in with
her. What did I say? I peed my pants!

TABBY. I don't know what to think anymore, I know I
can feel that he loves me, and I love him. I do
but every time we start to connect, he gets these
weirdo random tummy aches and runs off! I
hope he's not allergic to my family like Donald
was.

VINNY. I don't know why. Whenever I get close to her,
I get sick. No, it's not a coincidence. I've peed
my pants, I threw up in her mouth, and
something else happened at the fair. I can't tell
you, but I'm banned from the fair now! Don't
you see my body is telling me I'm not ready to
move on from Cali I still miss her my body is
rejecting Tabby.

TABBY. Maybe I should just give him some space?
But how much space does he need? And I have
needs too, I can't keep doing this. I need to find
out once and for all or I'm gonna go crazy.

VINNY. I can't see her anymore I have to break up
with her. I love her and she's all I think about
but if I keep seeing her, I think I'm gonna die.
(Hangs up phone.)

Scene 8

VINNY'S apartment (stage left). He's folding cat shelter laundry A knock on the door. He answers, it's TABBY.

TABBY. Are you busy?
VINNY. Yes. I'm folding laundry. You should go.

(Tabby enters anyway. He goes back to folding laundry.)

TABBY. I don't know if this is worth saving or not. Do you love me?
VINNY. Yes, I do!
TABBY. Then what's the problem?
VINNY. I can't see you anymore. I love you and I want to be with you. But I get sick every time I get close to you. You remind me of my ex, and I have all these feelings come up and I can't handle it, I guess. I just can't move on yet, I'm sorry I put you through this.
TABBY. That's why you run away every time? *(Pause.)* She would want you to move on.
VINNY. I know, I just can't. Honestly, I feel guilty how it ended.
TABBY. Well, what would you say to her if you could see her one more time?
VINNY. I never got to say goodbye.
TABBY. *(Takes out a bunch of psychic paraphernalia from her bag.)* I told you new age shit is real. *(Sets everything up on the coffee table.)*
VINNY. You can bring her back?

TABBY. I can bring your spirit back so you can talk to
her.

VINNY. Where did you learn this?

TABBY. Detroit... OK now our intentions need to be
pure and wholesome or else we could contact a
demon.

VINNY. Oh, cool what does that mean?

TABBY. We'll go to hell.

VINNY. Oh.

TABBY. *(Does her hocus pocus ritual thingamajig....)*
Calling all spirits from the spirit world. This is
Tabby! *(To Vinny.)* Her name's Cali? Is that her
full name?

VINNY. No, it's Calico.

TABBY. Huh?

VINNY. Like the cat.

TABBY. OK for this to work I need something of hers
to reach her. Do you have a picture, a letter she
wrote, article of clothing of hers? *(Vinny points
to Tabby's yellow beanie she's wearing. She's
shocked.)* This was her hat?!?!

VINNY. Yes, but that's not why I gave it to you. You
look so good in it!

TABBY. *(Offended, then gives him a "we'll deal with
this later" look and gets back to work. Talking
to spirits around her with crystal ball.)* I am
TABBY. TABBY OF THE MATERIAL
WORLD…TABBY CALLING CALICO…
CALICO!!

VINNY. What's happening??

TABBY. *(slightly frustrated)* Shhhhhh…. only real cats
are responding. *(She tries again.)* Calling
Calico come in Calico. Tabby calling
Calicoooo... *(Going down the wormhole so to*

speak. Staring in the crystal ball getting really into it.)

TABBY. I think I see her! Oh fuck! Meow! *(A possessed feral cat takes over her body. She has convulsions. A bunch of cat noises come out of Tabby's mouth. Feral meowing cat hisses in heat, whatever. She's struggling so the cat spirit doesn't take over. She finally sneezes and that causes the invisible spirit cat to bite tabby on the neck and then the cat spirit leaves her body.)* Ouch! You feral fucker! *(To Vinny)* I'm lucky I have cat allergies. OK there she is. Oh wow. Wow!! She really does look like me!

VINNY. Let me see!!

TABBY. Only I can see her. *(Ponders.)* Hmm I would never wear my hair like that though. Not in a million years. Way too long. *(To Vinny.)* Did you like that? Did you know ghost hair doesn't grow?

VINNY. Umm no.

TABBY. Yeah, so if you know when you're gonna die, oh which I can tell you later by the way, make sure you're happy with whatever hair you, you know-

VINNY. Can you still see her!?

TABBY. Oh yeah. Hold on. OK I see her!! Oh OK, she's busy. I can see her spirit. Hmm, OK be quiet! I'm communicating to her with my mind! *(She puts head to crystal ball. A KAPOW noise, and the whole experience is over. The lights go up.)*

VINNY. What happened?

TABBY. I couldn't bring her back now. She's busy
     taking a pottery class. Ordinarily I'd push
     through but it looks like a final exam.
VINNY. So now what?!
TABBY. I communicated with her, she's coming
     tonight at 3:00 AM, don't worry you'll be fine,
     but choose your words carefully. She'll only be
     back for a few minutes, she said she's happy to
     see you. *(She exits, while he hits his bong, lays
     down on couch, and falls asleep.)*

Scene 9

*VINNY is asleep on the couch there's loud
knocks on the door he is startled its only
midnight he opens the door it's CALI GHOST
and she barges in.*

CALI GHOST. Oh FUCK!!!
VINNY. Whoa...
CALI GHOST. I was just taking a pottery class with
     Clark Gable and Malcolm X!!! *(Vinny backs
     away.)* What? You knew I was coming.
VINNY. I thought you were coming at 3:00 AM.
CALI GHOST. That's spirit world time! Your dumb
     psychic friend didn't account for the time
     change! So, what the F is so important you had
     to... call me from heaven...mind you! To this
     litter box you call Earth!! Oh, this better be
     important! I was glazing an ashtray!
VINNY. Um... you've changed.
CALI GHOST. Well, geez Vinny I'm in the spirit world
     now! This fucking place sucks. I hate to tell

you Vinny, but I know a lot of shit. Did you
know Earth is hell?!
VINNY. What?
CALI GHOST. Oh, fuck I said too much. I better not
turn into a fucking person again, I gotta get
outta here. *(She heads towards the door.)*
VINNY. Cali wait!!
CALI GHOST. No fuck you! I have to finish my
ashtray! And if you ever summon me again, I'm
gonna make sure you go to Dark Hell that's
even worse than here!
VINNY. Cali I just wanted to say goodbye.
CALI GHOST. Goodbye loser! Now go to Hell! *(Evil
laugh.)*

Scene 10

*Next morning in TABBY'S apartment (stage
right.) Loud knocks on the door. She opens door
and it's VINNY.)*

TABBY. Umm hi... are you OK?
VINNY. No! I saw Calico, why did you say she was
happy to see me? Oh my gosh, she's a horrible
person... or ghost or whatever. She said I was
gonna go to hell if she didn't finish her ashtray!
Listen Tabby, I like you, but I was using you,
because I missed Cali, and I didn't even know
it. That's not fair. I'm so sorry, don't worry. I'll
get pizza somewhere else. Goodbye Tabby.
(Turns away to leave.)
TABBY. Vinny wait!
VINNY. What.

TABBY. I had a surprise for you. Here, take them both.
     (Tabby gives him an envelope with two tickets.)
VINNY. They're tickets to The Monkees!
TABBY. I got them because we had fun at the Burt
     Bacharach concert, and your birthday is coming
     up. I was gonna wait till your birthday, but you
     can have them now. Enjoy the concert, Vinny.
VINNY. *(Looks at the envelope they came in.)* What's
     this?
TABBY. That was your birthday envelope. I remember
     you told me how you like Japanese culture, so I
     was learning Japanese. That means happy
     birthday I love you in Japanese. And then on
     the other side it's The Monkee's logo, but in
     Japanese. And then a Buddhist, the floor below
     me, blessed it so it should give you good luck.
VINNY. Oh, noo…
TABBY. No please.
VINNY. No, you take it. You go to The Monkee's.
TABBY. No, you go I insist.
VINNY. No, you go you're too good for me.
TABBY. But you like Davy Jones.
VINNY. Honestly, I only said that because you said
     you like Davy Jones. Here you take them. *(He
     hands them over.)*
TABBY. No, you take them.
VINNY. No, you take them.
TABBY. *(Irritated)* No you take them.
VINNY. *(Turned on, flirty.)* No, you take them.
TABBY. *(plays along flirty)* No you take them.
VINNY. No, you take them.
TABBY. No, you take them.

BUDDHIST NEIGHBOR. *(voice-over)* Somebody
    take them or I'm retracting my Buddhist
    blessing I'm trying to sleep!!
VINNY. *(He takes them.)* Tabby, will you go to The
    Monkee's concert with me? Please don't say no.
    I want to get to know you, the real you. I'm
    sorry that I messed things up and got you
    involved. Can we start over? Please, it would
    mean a lot to me... *(Pause.)* hi my name's
    Vinny. *(A pause. They hug.)*

End of Play.

THE GATEKEEPER PARADOX
(Theatrical Version)

by Erin Hadfield

Overview
a 40-minute comedy
for 4 actors, 3 female and 1 any gender

Synopsis
The Gatekeeper Paradox is a metaphysical dark
comedy play, set outside the gates of Heaven, Hell, and
the In–Between. It is a heart–felt and comedic journey
for a kind woman named Abigail, who finds herself at
a cross road between these gates, aiming to convince
The Gatekeeper of her worthiness to enter into Heaven;
for more than just herself. Hijinks and twists will keep
audiences at the edge of their seat.

Characters
ABIGAIL – female, mid to late forties
SAMMY   – female, mid to late twenties
PETER   – female, 5,001
HAND

Setting
Heaven's Gate, the "INBETWEEN"
Time can be open or current

Notes
Abigail is wearing white silk pajamas and a white silk
robe; she should have a bag of gummie bears in her

pocket. Sammy is in a bright hot pink bikini, Jackie–O Sunglasses, and a giant sun hat. Peter will be in a white robe with a golden rope belt. NO SHOES for anyone. Hand is wearing a white glove and black tuxedo jacket with a white towel draped over their arm; should see up to his elbow. The sacred script book should be red, big, and golden pages.

Music Use Note

Licensees must secure permission for any copyrighted music or use only original music they own. All music clearances are the licensee's responsibility, and they agree to indemnify the copyright owners and licensing agent against any related claims.

Original Premiere

The Gatekeeper Paradox premiered on May 31st, 2025, at the 2025 Extravaganza One Act Fest. The production was directed by Wolfgang Bodison. The set design was by Erin Hadfield and Wolfgang Bodison.

Original Cast

ABIGAIL – Erin Hadfield
SAMMY   – Sophie Steele
PETER   – Lynette B. Garcia-Argueta
HAND   – Jose Doza

Performance Rights

This play may not be performed, reproduced, or adapted without written permission from the author. To request performance rights, please contact: E. Hadfield
TheGateKeeperParadox@gmail.com

Jose Doza, Lynette B. Garcia-Argueta,
Erin Hadfield, and Sophie Steele
photo by Ashley Elsa White

Scene 1

AC/DC's "Highway to Hell," begins blasting in the dark. Lights up. A bright white light comes up in a spot on a woman sleeping in what seems like a blanket of clouds. The woman awakens from a happy, dream like state, then suddenly is startled as she takes in the strange location and bed. ABIGAIL, sweet face and warm eyes. Abigail looks around puzzled trying to figure out where she is, when suddenly she looks over and sees an interesting young woman. SAMMY, is relaxing on a hot pink chaise lounge chair, on top of a platform slightly risen on a pillar with two or three stairs coming down. Should be white with clouds around and short enough that Abigail can reach her from standing below. She is holding a golden reflector as if suntanning, though there is clearly no sun; with a glowing star chart on the back. The glow can be seen in the dark for audience before lights come on. Abigail unsure quite what to do, walks over to Sammy.

ABIGAIL. *(Bit Loud)* Excuse me miss...

Sammy does not respond or even notice Abigail.

ABIGAIL. *(louder)* Excuse me Miss, I was...

The volume somehow rises, as Sammy sings along. Abigail yells at the top of her lungs.

ABIGAIL. Excuse me miss; I was wondering if you could please help me?

Surprised, Sammy pulls down her shades slightly. She snaps her fingers and the music shuts off, she then stares at Abigail, with a "yeah...what do you want already?" look.

ABIGAIL. Right. Well, I honestly am not sure where I am. I remember laying down for a moment to rest once my family headed out after brunch...and then I wake up here. *(pause)* Where ever here is. Doesn't feel like a dream.

Abigail notices a bright light shimmering off of a golden gate in the distance. Towards the audience for a smaller theater, or if big enough stage towards a large staircase with a gate at the top.

ABIGAIL. That's a strange place for a gate.

Abigail walks over and shakes the gate. Abigail pauses with realization. She hesitates for a moment then turns to Sammy, she braces herself.

ABIGAIL. ...is this heav–
SAMMY. *(oddly playful sympathy)*...Yeeaahhh.

Abigail then thinks for a brief moment.

ABIGAIL. Oh...so that means I'm–

SAMMY. Yeah. Sorry bout that. No heads up or
      anything, sometimes they do that. Kinda crappy
      if ya ask me...but they don't, so what can ya do.

      *Sammy puts her shades back on, snaps and the
      volume comes on full blast. Abigail, obviously
      hit by a lead weight, takes a few steps back in
      disbelief, trying to grapple with this
      information. Sammy peeks at her over her
      glasses at Abigail, who is now so sullen her
      legs begin to shake and she moves to sit.
      Sammy snaps her fingers and the music fades,
      and a chair suddenly appears, catching
      Abigail. This shakes Abby back, as she notices
      she is now sitting, and she looks up at Sammy,
      devastation in her eyes.*

ABIGAIL. I didn't get to say goodbye...

      *Sammy proceeds to go down the stairs off her
      pillar and walks over to Abigail, with as much
      empathy as she can muster.*

SAMMY. Look, I know it's tough, and leaving our
      loved ones is always the roughest part.

      *Sammy taps Abigail on the head, Abby trying to
      be polite smiles back in odd shock of her
      "comforting."*

SAMMY. But, you'll be okay and eventually so will
      they.

Sammy then tries to rub Abby's shoulders but is very rough, Abby winces in pain towards the audience without Sammy noticing as she tries to pull away but she still tries to remain sweet through her grief.

SAMMY. It's a part of the whole life and death rig–ama–row. I know it sucks, right?

Sammy begins to head back to her pillar lounge.

SAMMY. Though at least you got to head out as an older lady – led a pretty full life. I mean hey, they took my ass when I was crazy young so whatcha gonna do?

ABIGAIL. *(sincerely)* I'm sorry.

Sammy is slightly taken a-back that Abigail cares for her in this moment.

SAMMY. Ah, it's all good...thanks.

Abigail smiles, then looks down again in silence but slightly more at peace. Sammy takes this as a note of job done and snaps her finger, re–blasting her tunes. Abigail continues to sit for a moment.
Finally, Abigail looks to Sammy, who is now munching on a large extra cheese and olive pizza. Unsure of where that came from, she presses on. While Abby was at the gate, Sammy had knocked on the pillar, and a butler hand, in tuxedo with a white glove and white towel over

its arm popped out of nowhere (person hidden behind the pillar) and gave Sammy the pizza. (The hand is a very important character to this play.)

Abigail walks over to the gate and pauses, she mouths the name Amy, then has a brief moment with herself. With a new change, she walks over to Sammy ready to accept her fate. Abigail stares at Sammy until she snaps off the music again.

ABIGAIL. I'm Abigail, but my family calls me Abby.
SAMMY. Sammy.
ABIGAIL. Nice to meet you Sammy.

Sammy nods and snaps her fingers, tunes back on. Abigail begins staring at Sammy. Sammy a bit weirded out, tries to ignore this. Abigail keeps staring, Sammy brings up her magazine to cover her face, Abigail moves in closer, Sammy raises it higher, Abigail then begins to pull it down. Sammy freaks, startling Abigail. She snaps again and the music stops.

SAMMY. Woah...take a pic, it will last longer.
ABIGAIL. Sorry, sorry. It's just, your eyes, you look
     very familiar.

Sammy takes in Abigail quickly.

SAMMY. *(annoyed)* Yeah you too, but impossible so...

*Sammy snaps back on her music. Abigail
pauses – not sure what to do. She then looks
around and still unclear what to do next, goes
back to Sammy.*

ABIGAIL. *(loudly)* I'm sor...

*Abigail notices Sammy is not hearing her,
attempts to snap off the music herself. She tries
one hand, then the other, then both, and keeps
trying to snap with her back facing Sammy.
Sammy snaps it off, Abigail thinks she did it –
pleased, she turns back to Sammy who is now
glaring at her.*

ABIGAIL. Sorry to bother you again, but–
SAMMY. Yea, what is it? I am trying to relax ya know.
ABIGAIL. Right, again sorry. I was just wondering
     what I do now.
SAMMY. *(condescending)* You either go through the
     gates or ya don't. And if you don't, then that
     means you go...well, let's just say you'll get a
     great tan.

*Sammy points to a door that has been cloaked
in the darkness. It lights up red and a loud dun
dun dun noise bellows out, frightening Abby
who jumps behind Sammy's chair hanging on,
Sammy pushes her off.*

ABIGAIL. *(pointing at Heaven's Gate)* How do I go
     through those gates?
SAMMY. I check my list.
ABIGAIL. Great. *(beat)* Am I on the list?

Sammy gruffs, puts down her pizza, and knocks. The butler hand pops out with a giant red book with gold pages, from nowhere. As she lackadaisically flips through the pages, she scrolls down to a name with her finger, then closes the book.

SAMMY. Nope.

Sammy goes back to her relaxing and sunning, when she tries to snap her fingers again to put the music back on. Abigail grabs her hand to stop her.

ABIGAIL. Wait. There must be some mistake, Sammy, would you please check again?

Sammy pulls her hand away and reluctantly picks up the book, checks again. Abigail tries to peek over to see book, Sammy pulls it away.

SAMMY. Sorry Johnny, but like I said–the verdict is no.

Abigail begins to panic.

ABIGAIL. But I swear, I am a good person. *(beat to think)* I go to church.
SAMMY. Well...you go to church every so often, never during football Sundays, and only for the donuts.

Sammy knocks and the hands comes out with a beautiful fancy donut on a golden plate.

ABIGAIL. Football Sundays are family time, and
    some of my most cherished memories…

*Abigail notices the donut in Sammy's hand and
slightly goes for it, Sammy pulls it away and
takes a bite.*

ABIGAIL. …and they are delicious donuts.
SAMMY. Yeah…I bet. *(beat)* So we good here? You're
    exit is through that side.

She points to the ominous red door.

ABIGAIL. This can't be right. I was loving to my
    family and always supported each of them.

*Sammy sets down her donut and comes down
the stairs and begins to push Abigail towards
the red door. Who is pushing back, in a funny
slow slide across the floor.*

SAMMY. Yea I saw, which true not all parents do, but
    sadly, it's more complicated than that. So it's
    looking like you're gonna still have to take that
    downward toll.

*Abigail blocks the door and Sammy tickles her
away, then opens the door. Horrible hellish
sounds echo through the doorway while
illuminated flames appear. Sammy starts
pushing Abigail again towards the door,
Abigail desperately attempts to avoid this fate
as she ends up kind of backwards laying on top*

*of Sammy and struggling to shut the door;
when she finally succeeds.*

ABIGAIL. Please...I just don't understand. I was good.
I did good. I volunteered, I donated to my
grand-children's schools, brought lunches to the
homeless–

*The two catch their breath in sync with one
final breath together. They then stumble
towards the same chair from earlier while
catching their breath without seeing the other.*

SAMMY. *(interrupting)* Yeah, but didn't volunteering
end up with something good out the deal for
you too? So it wasn't really a selfless deed
wouldn't you say?

*Abby gets to the chair and sits slightly before
Sammy can, who looks at her annoyed but then
moves on.*

ABIGAIL. I...I don't...
SAMMY. Okay, I suppose I will explain it ya, but pay
attention cause I am only going to say it once,
capeesh?

*Abby sits quickly at attention and nods. Sammy
grabs the sacred book, looking up Abigail.*

SAMMY. You mentioned donating to your
grandchildren's school. Super nice of ya,
however Abby, because you gave money, your

grandchildren were given special privileges, were they not?

ABIGAIL. Nooooo.

SAMMY. *(mockingly snarking)* Oh...okay. By donating – you were made head of the PTA, which provided you with a certain coveted position in the school wouldn't you say?

ABIGAIL. I suppose it did, yes.

SAMMY. So maybe, just maybe, that helped out your grandkids, with all your relationships with the teachers, coaches, etcetera?

ABIGAIL. Again, I suppose maybe in some ways, but they earned all their achievements for working hard, and studying; not because I had friends.

SAMMY. If you say so. Moving on then, cause someone's still missing the point yeah? *(Beat)* Okay, this is kind of genius. What about the homeless you brought lunches to, wasn't that not also about getting rid of food YOU didn't like without your husband noticing?

ABIGAIL. Ohhh okay, just because I did not care for everything I put in their lunches, doesn't mean I didn't give them lunches. Or blankets when it was cold, or–

SAMMY. –righhhhhht...and when you did that, how did that make you feel?

ABIGAIL. Huh?

Sammy walks over to her pillar and knocks; the hand comes out with a cold coke.

SAMMY. When you gave– *(Sammy annoyed, knocks again, hand pops out with a straw and sticks it into her coke (okay if there is small struggle to do so))* –the homeless blankets or lunches, did all the blah blah blah. How did it make YOU feel Abigail?

ABIGAIL. It made me feel good! I admit it, I like people thinking I was a good person. I liked giving to others because it gave me joy knowing I was doing something for someone else. But is that really so wrong?

Abigail takes the coke as if Sammy was offering it to her, irritated, Sammy goes back and knocks, hand comes out with another coke – with a straw.

SAMMY. Well it's not really doing that good deed out of a self-less reason is it? So, how good does it actually make you? *(beat)* I mean, kinda seems to me like you're a narcissist who enjoys all eyes on her, and the question really then becomes would you have done those things if no one knew, or could give you your kudos?

ABIGAIL. *(pause)* I guess I never really thought of it like that.

Abigail turns towards Sammy, who takes her coke back from Abigail and proceeds to double fist drink her sodas.

SAMMY. See?

As Sammy is about to take a sip, Abigail stops her.

ABIGAIL. But I would like to believe that yes, I would
    have still done it. I mean there were times I
    gave without others knowing.
SAMMY. But ya still felt good about yourself right?
ABIGAIL. Yeah. It still felt good *(beat)* I guess I could
    have done more.
SAMMY. Maybe you could have. *(beat)* Anyway,
    close but no cigar as they say, and I am getting
    tired of explaining, so you can begin your trip
    down–

*Sammy turns to go back to her pillar; Abigail
gets her in her way. Sammy with anger
squeezes her sodas which spill onto ground.
Abigail goes to clean it up with Sammy's beach
towel. Sammy gives her a "what the hell do you
think you're doing?" eyes, Abigail shakes her
head no, and places the towel back and steps
aside, Sammy proceeds up to her lounge chair.*

ABIGAIL. No, listen Sammy. I did do things for others
    that weren't necessarily good for me.
SAMMY. Like what?
ABIGAIL. Um, I acted as a surrogate for my best
    friend who couldn't have a child on her own,
    which was incredibly difficult to carry a baby
    and give it to someone else; especially after
    losing...

*Abigail notices Sammy is not listening clear
enough as she replaces her towel on the lounge
chair, so Abigail grabs the towel and they
struggle with it.*

ABIGAIL. I tried to always take the high road and not step on others to get ahead. I was an honest person, and I was faithful to my husband. God Damn It I–

A loud thundering sound is heard. Abigail frightened leaps under the towel. Sammy eyes her, she is a little impressed. Abby carefully peeks out from the towel at Sammy and laughs awkwardly. Then hands the towel politely back to Sammy.

ABIGAIL. Gosh darn it, gosh darn it– *(pause)* I raised my children to be good people and never judge someone else for who they were on the outside.
SAMMY. Yea, pretty impressive stuff. Really, brava.
ABIGAIL. *(exasperated)* Then does none of that matter?
SAMMY. Look I know it doesn't make sense, but—
ABIGAIL. *(now yelling in a deepened voice, fully out of character and grabbing onto Sammy)* No, no, no. I did everything we were taught to do of right versus wrong; I stayed in the right. I knew I had to earn my place here to see her, I...I demand you find someone to fix this cause there has been a grave error! I am begging you!
SAMMY. *(pulling her off, standing up and coming down steps)* Woah...look, I really wish I could help you, I do, but you're just not getting it.

Sammy taps Abigail on the head.

ABIGAIL. Ugh, you are so exhausting!
SAMMY. Yeah well, whoever smelled it, dealt it.

ABIGAIL. What, that doesn't even make sense.
SAMMY. I know you are but what am I?
ABIGAIL. You are such a child!
SAMMY. Duhhhhhh.

The two turn their backs to one another, both in a huff with their arms crossed the same way. After a pause, Abigail turns back around with ease and sees Sammy cleaning the coke with her towel. Abby confused, presses on.

ABIGAIL. Please, I have to get into heaven, I have to see my little girl.
SAMMY. Your little girl?

Sammy begins looking through the book.

ABIGAIL. My third child, she passed away when she was just a baby and I never got to see her grow up. But she is in there and I have to see her, I need her to know that I never stopped loving her; and that I am so sorry.
SAMMY. I'm sorry, I hadn't realized.
ABIGAIL. Isn't it in your book?

Sammy nervously knocks and hands the book back to the hand, who takes it then throws it back out and it lands on the floor.

SAMMY. Well technically yeah, but this is only part of–
ABIGAIL. *(desperate)* Wait! I think I am starting to get it.

Sammy gives Abigail a please look. But Abby turns Sammy and pushes her butt back up onto her pillar. She then begins to make Sammy comfortable with all her things; sunglasses, magazine, suntan board, etc.

ABIGAIL. No really. *(beat)* I was human, I was human and I wasn't without making mistakes, and that some of those mistakes probably did hurt others. I cussed a lot, I cut people off in traffic– even if there was oodles of space in front of them, I caused the deat–

SAMMY. *(interrupting)* –Funny enough one of the purgatories, is just a giant replica of the 405 freeway in complete gridlock, and each car has no air conditioning and a broken radio.

ABIGAIL. Right... *(Abby offering Sammy soda, puts the straw in her mouth)* so, basically because we do good in life, if it stems from selfish reasons or to feel good about oneself, then it isn't a truly good deed. And I did many good deeds, but that doesn't make me automatically a good person and my mistakes.. *(pause of realization)*...my mistakes do not make me evil either.

SAMMY. Yeah, wow, someone is starting to use their brain.

Abigail is excited she has figured it out, and starts motioning for Sammy to open the gate.

SAMMY. Unfortunately for you, understanding partly is not enough; you must fully see. I mean if you really got it the doors would just open, so...

Sammy realizes she said too much.

ABIGAIL. Wha..aaa...t do you mean, they'll just open? *(beat)* Aren't you the gate keeper?

Sammy and Abby look towards gate, then back at each other, then back at gate, then as they look back at each other again, Sammy begins to stammer off.

ABIGAIL. But...I...

Abigail takes off towards the gate entrance.

ABIGAIL. AMY!!!

Right as she reaches the gate, Sammy is trying to pull her off. Suddenly another door, with a blue sign over it that reads "Inbetweens" flies open. Both girls are startled backwards. Abby runs and hides.
In walks Peter (thousands of years old), she carries a magazine under arm and looks exhausted and sweaty. Sammy doesn't move out of Peter's way.

PETER. Whewwww. Chili tuesdays – not okay. *(beat)* Sammy!?!
SAMMY. Petra–
PETER. I have told you several times it is Peter.
SAMMY. Right, sure–sure. PEEETTTEEERRRR, got it. How's that chili treatin' ya?

Peter stares at Sammy, like an angry principal, then pushes Sammy out of her way and goes over to the pillar and knocks. Hand comes out with a large medicine cup of pink liquid. Peter downs it.

PETER. Mmmm hmm. Anyway, I asked you to simply keep an eye on things while I...mmmm...

Peter knocks again. Hand comes out with bottle of Pepto and refills the cup. Peter downs it again. Abby comes out of hiding.

PETER. ...while I ran to the restroom, not to anoint yourself gate queen. *(to self)* 5,000 years old, and yet you will be what gives me gray hair.
SAMMY. Your hair doesn't gray and I am sorry, but there is a really important reason this time.
PETER. There is always an important reason Sammy.

Peter notices the book on the floor.

PETER. Don't tell me you took one of the sacred life evidence scripts?

Sammy pulls her shades down and tries to run behind Abigail; Abby freaked out not sure what to do or who this is, but then Sammy pushes Abigail towards Peter.

PETER. Something, every time. *(sighs)* I'm very sorry Abigail, Sammy is um...spirited.
ABIGAIL. *(still freaked)* I don't understand what's happening.

PETER. I'm Peter, the gate keeper to Heaven.

A calm settles over Abigail, she looks back at Sammy, who avoids her.

ABIGAIL. Oh, I see.

Peter signals Abigail to walk over to the side with her as she "whisper" explains.

PETER. Yeah, I um, had to run to the bathroom really quick; mmmm, the chili up here has quite the kick. And everyone up here was really having a moment, so I had to use the port-o-potty over there in the in–between...well...anyway–

Peter then tries to go after Sammy. They then begin circling round Abby who tries to keep up and ends up very dizzy.

PETER. Sammy here was just supposed to ask anyone who came up in the meantime to wait until I returned; though she can never help herself from mischief. Usually it's sneaking inside the gate, now it is pretending to be the gate keeper.
ABIGAIL. Sneaking in? She isn't allowed in?

Abby dazed from spinning, wonders over and tries to steady herself.

PETER. No, Sammy is an in-between. She's grown up here, outside the gate.
ABIGAIL. An in-between?

SAMMY. So rude, you know I hate being called
      that...Petra.

Peter looks at Sammy with a watch it look.

PETER. Why do you keep doing this? *(beat)* You are
      pretty resourceful I will give you that. But this
      is getting out of hand Sammy, you took a
      sacred script this time.
SAMMY. *(annoyed)* Look Petra.

Peter gives a look.

SAMMY. Sorry, Peter. I get it, I shouldn't have taken
      the sacred thingie-a-magigie. But...I helped
      Abby here admit that she made mistakes. She
      now understands that doing a good deed is not
      without selfishness, except well the small
      things. But I–
PETER. *(heavy sigh)* Sammy–
SAMMY. Okay before you Sammy me, I saw on her
      notes that–
PETER. Wait! How did you see her notes?

*Peter chases Sammy away from the pillar.
While they are doing this, Abigail goes over
and decides to try knocking herself. The hand
pops out with an oversized pink sprinkled
donut. Abigail's eyes light up and she digs in.
Trying not to reveal to Sammy and Peter.*

SAMMY. Um...um...um... *(super–fast)* I saw on her
      notes that she needed to come to the realization
      that good deeds out of selfish reasons do not

make you automatically good, that she was human and needed to humble herself to confess her sins, and by doing so she could actually help change her ruling. *(mockingly and back to normal pace)* "To humble oneself before him."

Peter and Abigail look at Sammy impressed.

SAMMY. Gotta love that Indiana, taught me all I know... *(pause)* Indiana Jones and the Last Crusade...

Peter stares at Sammy.

SAMMY. Come on Peter it was played for the last movie night, you caught me right afterwards? Didn't even let me keep my gummy bears? Which was totes uncool.

Abby shakes her head. Still no reaction from Peter.

PETER. That was kind of you to help someone other than yourself, truly shows a lot of growth for you I must say.
SAMMY. Thanks?
PETER. However, you interpreted her notes wrong Sammy, that's what I was trying to tell you before you cut me off.

Sammy tries to grab the book; Peter pulls it away.

SAMMY. No, they said.

PETER. I know what they said. But that was her own
          personal judgements on herself, she needed to
          change her own ruling of herself.
SAMMY. I don't understand.

Abigail turns around, face in donut.

ABIGAIL. Me either?

They notice the donut; she tries to hide it.

PETER. It's simple really. Mmmmm.

*Peter farts terribly, and goes towards the pillar
as Sammy and Abby deal with horrible stench.
Abby politely, Sammy not so much. Peter
knocks and this time, the hand gives her the full
bottle, she chugs it then turns back to Abigail.*

PETER. Abigail – you are your own prosecutor,
          torturing yourself on whether you deserve to
          enter because you still have not forgiven
          yourself for what happened to your daughter.
ABIGAIL. Amy?
PETER. Yes. You blame yourself. But deep down you
          know it was not your fault. So you did all this
          good, but to try to convince yourself you were
          good and would be deserving to enter Heaven.
ABIGAIL. I...

*During their conversation, Sammy walks over
to the pillar, knocks and hand comes out with
bottle of Febreeze, Sammy sprays it towards
Peter.*

ABIGAIL. It was my fault, I shouldn't have...

Abigail goes silent. Sammy goes over and takes her by the hand, Abigail is grateful.

PETER. Abigail, look at me. It is not your fault, and if you do not forgive yourself, you, like Sammy; will be an in-between. Sorry, Sammy.

ABIGAIL. What do you need to forgive yourself for?

PETER. She doesn't.

ABIGAIL. I don't understand, I thought an in–between needed–

SAMMY. Petra here...

PETER. Peter! It is a family name and I am very proud of it.

SAMMY. Peter says I am waiting. But for what I don't know, and until I choose to stop waiting I can't stay in there. Though I think she just doesn't like me and so she throws me out.

PETER. Sammy, you don't know because you refuse to open your heart.

SAMMY. Bor–ing. I am so over the yada yada, mumbo gumbo. I am not waiting for anything, except maybe more gummy bears.

ABIGAIL. Oh, I actually have some gummy bears.

At the same time

SAMMY. You do?!
PETER. You do?!

Abigail pulls out a bag of gummy bears.

ABIGAIL. Yeah, I always carry some in my pocket, even when I nap; they're actually my favorite too. Here you go Sammy, they're all yours.
SAMMY. Thanks...you rock Abby! First person to not totally suck up here. No offense Petey.
PETER. Peter!
SAMMY. Wasn't Petra.

Peter gives her a funny look, trying not to laugh as she actually finds this humorous.

PETER. Have you ever thought that maybe you are waiting cause you were trying to protect, help someone.
SAMMY. *(more serious for first time)* Um hello McPetey! I am trying to help someone, right now, helping Abby here get into Heaven.
PETER. You did help...

Sammy looks proud. Abby gets excited at the prospect of entering Heaven; finally. They inflate together.

PETER. ...To a degree.

Sammy and Abby deflate together.

SAMMY. Always a catch. *(to Abby)* They love a good catch up here. *(back to Peter)* What, are ya going to do, put me in purgatory Petey?
PETER. It's Peter!
SAMMY. Petey, Petra, Petra-a-runi, Pete-a-tron, Petrina, Pella Pella, Petrialacious, Petroula–
ABIGAIL. *(cutting Sammy off)* –Sammy!

Sammy stops and looks down like kid embarrassed.

PETER. No Sammy, no purgatory; other than the one you are doing to yourself.

ABIGAIL. This is all too much, what happened to extending grace?

PETER. I understand your instinct to protect Sammy, but she has had several chances and she refuses to let go.

ABIGAIL. Can't you make an exception, or tell her exactly how to do it?

PETER. Doesn't work that way.

ABIGAIL. Well that's poppy-cock, excuse my French.

Peter taken aback; Sammy impressed.

PETER. Hey, he is listening...

As Peter and Abby continue to engage, Sammy goes over and tops her pizza with gummy bears and digs in.

ABIGAIL. Sorry, it just seems to me, that since this is Heaven and all you wouldn't have to jump through hoops. Why can't you simply tell a person what it is they need to do in order to go through the gates?

PETER. It's not about knowing what to do Abigail. It is in YOU, you have to let go of your own darkness before you can move forward. Sometimes you have to let go and your path will become clear. And I believe I told you exactly what you needed to do, it's just whether you choose to hear it and do it. Just as I was specific with Sammy.

ABIGAIL. Well evidently not clear enough!

SAMMY. Stop! Stop fighting over what I need, I am standing right here...absolutely ridic... *(beat)* Abby, I appreciate what you're doing, but you got your probs too and I still don't know what it is I am waiting for, sooo honestly, I'm over it. *(to Peter)* I don't want to be in your stuffy old Heaven anyways. I'm going.

Sammy stomps off like a toddler.

ABIGAIL. No Sammy, wait.

SAMMY. It's fine, I'll just sneak in again some other time. *(she gives Abby a wink)* Nice to meet 'cha Abby. *(pause)* Man you're right, you do look so familiar. Anyway, ta–ta.

Sammy exits through the in–between door as Abby calls after her.

ABIGAIL. Nice to meet you Sammy. Hope to see you soon, well, in there hopefully.

Sammy pops back out.

SAMMY. Catch me later Pete–ies.

Sammy snaps her finger and we hear Phil Collins' "I don't care anymore" and she disappears again. Abigail smiles at the song lyrics, but then is overtaken by worry, Peter notices. Peter snaps off the music.

PETER. She'll be okay Abigail, she grew up here
          outside the gates.
ABIGAIL. Grew up? We continue to age up here.
PETER. We all age, I am 5,001, but in-betweens age
          like humans on earth because they are stuck
          half there and half here. Though humans also
          look different here than they did on earth; it's a
          whole thing.
ABIGAIL. Are there other in-betweens?
PETER. Yes. Those unable to let go or forgive
          themselves roam the void between Heaven and
          Earth.
ABIGAIL. How long has Sammy–
PETER. Twenty-six years.

Abigail looks back at the in-between door.

ABIGAIL. The poor thing. She is such an energetic
          spirit.
PETER. Yeah, sure.
ABIGAIL. I wish there was something I can do for
          her?
PETER. There is Abby.

Abigail turns back with hope.

ABIGAIL. What? Anything?
PETER. Forgive yourself, and enter the gates.
ABIGAIL. *(deflated)* But I...How will that help
          Sammy?
PETER. Sometimes we don't see the mark we leave on
          others, but it doesn't mean what we do didn't
          leave one. And trust me, Sammy seeing you

forgive yourself and go through, may help her
more than you can imagine.

*Abigail is unsure, she wants to enter Heaven
and wants to help Sammy, but she feels so
guilty.*

PETER. Abigail, what happened to Amy would have
        happened even if you were there. It was her
        time.
ABIGAIL. I was making a difference, she was getting
        better, than–
PETER. Abby, you have to stop blaming yourself. You
        did nothing wrong.
ABIGAIL. I don't think I can. *(pause)* I am so sorry
        Amy.
PETER. She knows.
ABIGAIL. How can she?
PETER. She knows. Forgive yourself.

*Abigail breathes heavy and then looks towards
where Sammy left.*

ABIGAIL *(to herself)* I am human, and I made
        mistakes. *(beat)* Thanks Sammy.

*Abigail walks to center stage; or to the golden
gates.*

ABIGAIL. Amy, I hope you will be able to forgive me,
        because I am so sorry baby girl, but I have to
        forgive myself now. It's the only way to see
        you, and I won't let you down again. I love you.

Mama's here now, and we will finally be together, my Sweet Amy.

Sounds of the gate opening and heaven's bright sparkling light come through with beautiful music. Abigail rushes to Peter, hugging her tightly and spinning her.

PETER. Woah, that's quite the hug.
ABIGAIL. Thank you Peter. Please, take care of Sammy and help her let go. I will be back to check on her as soon as I find Amy.

Peter smiles. Abigail heads towards the gate. As she reaches the gate, she sees Sammy peeking through the other door. Abigail turns to Peter, gives her a wave, then Peter turns to grab the book; or pizza. As she does so, Abigail waves Sammy over, who runs towards her quietly and the two share an exciting silent scream and go in together. Peter turns in time to see the back of them. She just smiles and shakes her head. The gate closes.

PETER. *(to hand)* Job well done.

Hand gives thumbs up.

PETER. I wonder if they'll figure it out...but, nobody looks how they did on earth. *(laughing to self)*

Peter picks up a slice of pizza and gives one to hand as she lays on the lounge chair.

PETER. Definitely like mother, like daughter.

> *Peter and the hand dab it out, she then snaps
> and Meghan Trainor's "MOM" turns on. She
> closes her eyes and takes a bite.
> Fade to black.*

End of Play

JUST PULL

by Niki J. Borger

Overview
a 10-minute drama
for 4 actors, 3 female, 1 male, and 1 female VO

Synopsis
Torn between justice and revenge, a young mother must decide whether or not to kill the woman who is responsible for her child's death.

Characters
SUI   – female, 20s to 30s
IRA   – female, 20s to 30s
NOXA   – female, 20s to 30s
STEVE – male, 20s to 30s, Sui's neighbor
LILY   – female, 3-5, VO

Setting
Present day. A small living room. Lonely children's toys litter the room. Days old, barely touched food sits on the table. In the very center, a single chair with a hostage on it.

Notes
Lily's line is optional and should only be included if you can record it from a child of an adequate age. It should not be done live, but played as an ethereal voice-over.

There's the option to include an actual gunshot at the end. That decision should be made by the director.

Original Premiere

Just Pull premiered on June 1st, 2025, at the 2025 Extravaganza One Act Fest, directed by Wolfgang Bodison.

Original Cast

SUI   – Niki J. Borger
IRA   – Megan Corse
NOXA   – Ashley Elsa White
STEVE – RC Lehman

Performance Rights

This play may not be performed, reproduced, or adapted without written permission from the author. To request performance rights, please go to https://nikijborger.com/plays

Niki J. Borger, RC Lehman, Ashley Elsa White, Megan Corse,
photo by Grant Terzakis

Scene 1

Lights up on a single empty chair in the middle of a family's living room. Eerie silence. Lights down.

Scene 2

Outside the door, the rattling from keys can be heard. The door opens and reveals SUI. The hallway behind her is lit. She picks up a paper bag when the building door down the hall opens. STEVE enters the hallway (o.s.) and sees Sui immediately.

STEVE. Hey Susanna.
SUI. Oh, hi STEVE.

Steve approaches Sui so they both stand in the doorway.

STEVE. How are you? Haven't seen you in a few.
    Everything okay?
SUI. Fine.
STEVE. You seem a little off. How's the new
    therapist? Do you feel like you're making
    progress?
SUI. She gave me a new prescription.
STEVE. That's nice. Is it making you feel any better?
SUI. It's okay.
STEVE. Okay… Oh, did you still want me to fix your
    heater? I have time now.
SUI. Now's not a good time, but thank you.

STEVE. What about your sink, is it still clogged? Also, I heard your washer a couple of days ago, and it was really loud. I think it's not balanced out evenly; that's why it makes so much noise. I could take a look–

SUI. Not now, but thank you.

STEVE. Okay.

SUI. I should get these in the fridge.

Sui starts closing the door on him.

STEVE. Of course. You look really nice today. It's good seeing you.

SUI. Thanks.

Sui closes the door on him. As it's closed, she leans against it and takes some deep, steadying breaths. Lights down.

Scene 3

A single spotlight on Sui at a kitchen counter. She starts unpacking the groceries from the bag when she comes across Lily's favorite cookies. Within a second, all the dark thoughts she's fighting so hard to repress take control of her again. She slams her fist onto the table, pulls a gun from the grocery bag, and directs it towards the center of the room. As all lights go up, they reveal NOXA tied to the chair in the center, hood-bagged, unconscious. At the same moment, IRA steps out of the dark and starts talking to Sui.

IRA. Do it.

Sui raises the gun.

IRA. Before someone finds us here.

Sui straightens her arm.

IRA. This is the chance you've been waiting for!

Sui moves in closer.

IRA. It's now or never. Just fucking do it!

Sui turns away her head so as not to see what she's about to do. She takes a deep breath in, then-

SUI. I can't!

The tension evaporates.

SUI. I can't. I'm sorry.

Sui sets the gun down on the counter. With shaking hands, she helps herself to some water.

SUI. Not here, anyway.
IRA. I can't believe you're chickening out now.
SUI. I'm not chickening out.
IRA. You're a coward.
SUI. That's not fair! I got us a gun!
IRA. Admit, you don't have the guts to do it.
SUI. It's not that easy to kill someone.

IRA. We've come this far, and now you're chickening
      out!
SUI. We've taken it far enough, okay.
IRA. No, we haven't! She's still breathing!
SUI. Barely!
IRA. *(loudly)* She killed your daughter for chrissake!

> *Sui and Ira both get emotional. Sui moves to a
> dresser and starts searching its drawers.*

IRA. And now you're just letting her get away with it.
SUI. We'll hand her over to the police. They'll know
      what to do.
IRA. The police will just let her go. Again.
SUI. There's more evidence now. Maybe this time
      she'll get what she deserves.
IRA. Right. Cause bad people always do.
SUI. We have to trust that they'll do the right thing.
IRA. Trust? This is too important to rely on trust!
SUI. They'll find out she's guilty, and they'll lock her
      away.

> *This sets Ira off.*

IRA. Lock her away? That's not enough!
SUI. Keep it down!
IRA. *(full volume)* She doesn't deserve to live!
SUI. SHH!
IRA. *(even louder)* She is a murderer! She killed–

> *From the corridor, the opening of a door can be
> heard. Then footsteps. Sui covers Ira's mouth to
> keep her from talking. Ira and Sui both listen
> for the neighbor to leave. When the building*

door has closed, Sui releases Ira.

IRA. She killed a 3-year-old child! That kind of person
    has no right to live!
SUI. Maybe it was an accident!

Sui listens to the door to make sure he's gone.

IRA. Come on, you don't believe that!
SUI. Maybe I do.

*Sui proceeds to Noxa, tightening the (non-
existent) cable ties around her wrists and
ankles.*

IRA. You're lying to yourself–
SUI. I'm not–
IRA. cause you're too much of a coward to face the
    truth!
SUI. I'm not a coward!
IRA. She is the reason Lily is dead!
SUI. Don't say her name, please.
IRA. Lily! Do you remember the milky smell of her
    head? And the hazel color of her eyes. And her
    rosy cheeks. And then suddenly they were
    white-
SUI. Stop it.
IRA. Way too white-
SUI. I said stop it!

Sui reaches for the gun on the kitchen counter.

IRA. And her lips all bl-
SUI. That's enough!

Sui points the gun at Ira's face.

IRA. What's wrong with you?

> *Sui realizes what just happened. She puts the gun back on the counter.*

SUI. I'm sorry. I just… can't… think straight. Everything's a blur.

> *Ira puts an arm around Sui. Sui speaks the italic words at the same time as Ira.*

IRA. I understand. I loved her too, you know.
SUI. *Loved…*
IRA. And I swore that I would not settle until *justice* was served.
SUI. *Justice…* Where's the justice in taking one life for another? You want revenge.
IRA. To me, there's no *difference* anymore.
SUI. The *difference…*
IRA. I'd rather die for justice than live with *regret.*
SUI. *Regret.*

> *Ira starts whispering in Sui's ear.*

IRA. Imagine we just let her walk, and she goes and accidentally kills someone else. Now it would be our fault as well. The blood would be on our hands. It would be on our conscience. We would look at ourselves and see nothing but a murderer. Could you live with that?
LILY. *(voice-over)* Mommy? Mommy, I'm waiting for you.

Noxa starts stirring.

IRA. The bitch is waking up.
SUI. Crap.

Sui breaks away from Ira.

IRA. We have to do it now.
SUI. I really don't think I can.
IRA. Then let me do it.
SUI. Quiet-
IRA. *(quieter)* Please! Let me do it!

Ira follows Sui, forcing Sui to deal with her.

SUI. I don't want you to become a killer.
IRA. I don't care! I just want it done!
SUI. You're not a bad person!
IRA. I hate you!
SUI. I know you're in pain, but–
IRA. I hate everything!
SUI. This is not the way!

Finally, Sui shoves Ira away. Ira releases her anger by turning away and screaming. Sui screams at the same time. Both Ira and Sui cover their mouths instantly. Outside the door, footsteps can be heard. Then a knock at the door. Neither Ira nor Sui dares to move.

SUI. Who is it?
STEVE. It's Steve. I heard… a commotion... everything alright?
SUI. Yes, everything's fine, thank you.

A moment.

STEVE. Do you need anything?
SUI. I'm okay.
STEVE. Okay.

The neighbor leaves, and his door closes.

IRA. You're a liar and a coward! What would Lily
       say–
SUI. Don't you dare use her against me! If Lily could
       see this, she would be so scared. She always
       saw the best in us, and look what we've
       become! Turned against one another like
       maniacs! Lying to our friends! Having a gun! In
       our apartment! This is insane!

*Noxa raises her head and gives a groan. Ira
attempts to punch her, but Sui keeps getting in
the way.*

SUI. Maybe we should hear what she has to say.
IRA. I don't want to!

Ira shoves the groceries off the table.

SUI. This is wrong. All of this is wrong.
IRA. Everything's been wrong since she's gone. This is
       your chance to fix it.
SUI. But there is no fixing it.
IRA. Yes, there is.
STEVE. Susanna, I heard something break. I'm really
       worried.
IRA. That pain you're feeling, for Lily, I feel it too.

STEVE. Can you say something, please?
IRA. That loss. All these moments when you should
hear her laugh, or cry, or yell Mommy, but then
there's only the everlasting silence of these
walls – I have them, too.
STEVE. Unless you say something, I'm gonna let
myself in to check on you.
IRA. But this, right here, this will make it go away.
Forever. And she will get what she deserves.
STEVE. Like we discussed. Okay?
SUI. Lily won't come back to life.
IRA. Maybe not. But we would finally be at peace.
SUI. There is no peace without Lily.
IRA. Exactly.

*As they look at each other, Sui and Ira finally
understand one another. Sui takes the gun and
raises it at Noxa's head, just as Ira rips off the
pillowcase. They confront her together.*

STEVE. Okay, I'm coming in.
SUI. *(to Noxa)* Why did you do it?

Noxa doesn't answer.

STEVE. *(to Sui)* It was not your fault!

*Steve only has eyes for Sui and slowly starts
closing in.*

IRA. *(to Noxa)* Why did you go inside?
SUI. *(to Noxa)* Why did you let her out of sight?
IRA. *(to Noxa)* Why weren't you with her that minute?
STEVE. *(to Sui)* It was an accident!

IRA. *(to Noxa)* Why did you give her a kiddie pool?
SUI. *(to Noxa)* Why didn't you check how much water
    was in there?
IRA. *(to Noxa)* Why didn't you hear her slip?
STEVE. *(to Sui)* It could've happened to anybody!
IRA. *(to Noxa)* Why did you have a kid in the first
    place?
SUI. *(to Noxa)* Why did you think you could be a
    mother?
IRA. *(to Noxa)* Why did you make her grow up with
    only one parent?
STEVE. *(to Sui)* You did the best you could!
IRA. *(to Noxa)* Why did you go inside?
SUI. *(to Noxa)* Why didn't you pay more attention?

Ira turns on Sui and starts addressing her.

IRA. *(to Sui)* Why didn't you know how to help her?
STEVE. *(to Sui)* Susanna, you don't have to do this!
IRA. *(to Sui)* Why did it take you so long to call an
    ambulance?
STEVE. *(to Sui)* I will help you get through this!
IRA. *(to Sui)* Why are you such a monster?
STEVE. *(to Sui)* Lily would want you to live!
NOXA and SUI. Please let me die!
IRA. *(to Sui)* Just pull!
STEVE. *(to Sui)* NO!

Steve lunges for the gun. All goes black.

Scene 4

Lights back up. Sui is sitting in the chair,

crying, holding the gun which is directed at her own head. Steve is holding it also. Noxa and Ira have disappeared. Slowly, Steve takes the gun from Sui's hands and slides it away. He pulls his phone and dials 911.

STEVE. I want to report an attempted suicide.

Lights slowly fade to black.

End of play.

LAUGH TRACK

by Megan Corse

Overview

a 23-minute comedy
for 5 actors, 2 female and 3 male

Synopsis

Expecting an intimate evening with her on-again off-
again boyfriend, Anne's world is turned upside down
as she's taunted by a familiar and peculiar sound.

Characters

ANNE	– female, 30s, the down-on-her-luck hero
JOHN	– male, 30s, the boyfriend
DAVID	– male, 30s, the best friend
MONICA	– female, 20s, the new girlfriend
LUKE	– male, 30s, the mysterious twin brother

Setting

John's apartment at night, any Midwestern City, USA.

Notes

Takes place in modern day. A play that's referential of
sitcoms, film noir, and famous movies. To set the tone,
it's recommended to use sitcom-inspired opening
music, and because of the final *It's A Wonderful Life*
reference, 1940's closing music.

Original Premiere

Laugh Track premiered on May 31st, 2025, at the 2025 Extravaganza One Act Fest, directed by Wolfgang Bodison.

Original Cast

ANNE   – Megan Corse
JOHN   – RC Lehman
DAVID   – Kyle Tran
MONICA   – Ruju Dani
LUKE   – John O'Brien

Performance Rights

This play may not be performed, reproduced, or adapted without written permission from the author. To request performance rights, please contact Megan Corse at https://megancorse.com/contact.

RC Lehman, Kyle Tran, Megan Corse, and Ruju Dani,
photo by Grant Terzakis

Scene 1

Lights up in blue to indicate outdoors, nighttime. A doorway is downstage left at an angle. Anne, thirties, is pacing downstage and talking on her phone, looking nervous.

ANNE. Well of course I'm here, John hasn't called me in two weeks, then suddenly he invites me over? (*Listens*) No, we never broke up. Things are great between us. (*Listens*) So what if he missed my birthday, his twin brother, Luke, was in town. Can you imagine two of John? Ow, ow! Anyway, he made up for it. We took that trip to New York for Valentine's Day. We went to the 9/11 Museum. It was so romantic! (*Listens*) I see my friends all the time. (*Listens*) Like, at the bars where John's band is playing. (*Listens)* No, I didn't get a comped ticket. (*Listens)* No, I didn't get any drink tickets. (*Listens*) No, I didn't get a front row seat. (*Listens*) Ok, Mom, stop! This really isn't the time to dissect my life. (*Listens*) I'm fine! I love you too. Talk to you soon. Bye!

She hangs up, turns on her selfie camera to check makeup and hair, then knocks. Full lights up, dance music plays. It's startlingly bright, everything is very neat and colorful, like a sitcom. A cabinet and bar cart are downstage right, a dining room table with chairs is stage left. Upstage center are a couch and coffee table. John, thirties, handsome and knows it, stands from the couch to answer the door, wearing his guitar. David, thirties, and Monica, twenties, are talking on the couch, friendly with one another. All dressed in colorful clothes.

JOHN. Hey Annie.
ANNE. Hey, John.
JOHN. You made it.
ANNE. Mm-hm.
JOHN. It's good to see you. You look great.
ANNE. Thanks, um, you too. How have you-
JOHN. Come on in. Everyone else is here.
ANNE. What? Ev-everyone?

Anne steps through the door. David rises from the couch while John moves to join Monica upstage.

DAVID. Look what the cat dragged in!

David beelines to Anne and hugs her.

ANNE. H-hi, David. Wha-
DAVID. It's good to see you too, Anne!

David squeezes her tighter. Anne struggles to pull away.

ANNE. David? David…David!

Anne pushes him away. A laugh track sounds. Anne looks around, startled. She sees John and Monica.

DAVID. Anyone want a drink? Anne?

ANNE. Uh-
JOHN. Oh. Anne, this is Monica (*pronounced MOH-nica*).
ANNE. I'm sorry?
MONICA. Moh-nica.

She extends a limp hand for Anne to shake.
Anne looks at it.

ANNE. Moh-ni-ca?
MONICA. Well, not the hand, me.

Laugh track sounds again.

ANNE. What the-?
JOHN. Moh-nica, this is Anne.
MONICA. It's nice to finally meet you.
ANNE. Is it?
MONICA. Yes!
ANNE. Really?
MONICA. Of course!
ANNE. Ok.
MONICA. Ok!
ANNE. Why?
MONICA. Because it is!

Laugh track.

ANNE. What is that?!
DAVID. Anne, how about that drink?

John and Monica make excuses to leave while
giving David a "thumbs up" and "go for it"

*encouragement. They exit through the upstage
left door that leads to the rest of the apartment.*

ANNE. (*incensed*) What the fuck?
DAVID. What?
ANNE. What do you mean, "what"? Who the hell is
    she?
DAVID. That's Moh-nica.
ANNE. Yeah, so I heard. But who the hell is he?
DAVID. I don't know. I thought you were his
    girlfriend.
ANNE. So did I.
DAVID. Oh.

Laugh track.

ANNE. Do you hear that?!
DAVID. Hear what? Vodka soda, right?
ANNE. Have I just walked into an alternate universe? I
    must be losing my mind.

Anne drinks, then gags.

ANNE. What is this?

Laugh track.

ANNE. (*scared*) So it's a funny drink?
DAVID. When did you guys break up?
ANNE. Uh, last I checked, we hadn't. He's just been
    really distant lately, keeps saying he's busy,
    canceling dates last minute. I thought tonight
    was him coming to his senses, like to maybe
    apologize…or see me naked.

Laugh track. Anne starts drinking defiantly.

DAVID. Hey, maybe this is for the best, huh?

Anne drains her drink. Laugh track.

ANNE. (*mockingly*) Ha ha ha ha!
DAVID. Are you ok? Maybe we just need to get
    drunk.
ANNE. Moh-nica? Are you kidding me? What kind of
    stupid name is that?
DAVID. I'm pretty sure it's just Monica pronounced
    with pretension. He's an idiot, just for the
    record. Here, let's drink these and you'll be
    fine.

He pours them a shot and they drink.

ANNE. Last I checked, he's your best friend, Davey
    boy.
DAVID. Hey, I don't discriminate. I'm happy to be
    friends with the mentally deficient.

Laugh track.

ANNE. Wow. It must be me. I've completely lost it.

*Anne drinks, but the glass is empty. She licks
the glass and tries to get every last drop. Laugh
track.*

DAVID. We're friends, right?

ANNE. (*more scared*) Yeah, of course. Pour us another. Thanks to John, you've become one of my favorite people.

DAVID. Right, see? So-so things aren't all bad. I mean, there's other fish in the sea… You just have to open your eyes to what's right in front of you.

ANNE. You're right!

Anne gestures wildly with her glass in hand, drenching David. Laugh track. David gets up to clean himself off.

ANNE. I'm not standing up for myself. I'm letting him have the upper hand. Well no more. I'm taking control of this situation. John! (*to David*) You ok?

DAVID. Yeah. Peachy.

Laugh track. Monica enters.

ANNE. (*terrified*) John!

MONICA. Whoa.

ANNE. Oh, sorry.

MONICA. (*to David*) You ok?

DAVID. Yeah. Peachy.

Laugh track. David exits.

MONICA. Anne, do you have a second?

ANNE. S-sure.

MONICA. I just wanted to say, I think it's really great that you and John are still friends and can hang out like this.

ANNE. Oh?

MONICA. I mean, I don't know if I could handle it, if I were in your shoes.

ANNE. Mm-hm.

MONICA. He's just such a sweet, attractive guy. Who wouldn't want to stay friends with him, right?

ANNE. Right. That is so true! What. A. Guy.

MONICA. Anyway, I hope we can become friends too because I know all of his friends really like you…especially David.

ANNE. Uh-huh. Yeah.

MONICA. Really? Oh my god! Yes!

Monica suddenly jumps on Anne, hugging and straddling her. Laugh track.

MONICA. That makes me so happy. I know because John loves you, I will too. Oh, we should go on a double-date sometime!

ANNE. What?

Laugh track.

MONICA. You know, like the four of us. It was just a thought, no pressure.

Laugh track. Anne pushes Monica off of her.

ANNE. John!

MONICA. I'll go get him for you.

Laugh track keeps going as Monica hurriedly exits.

ANNE. Shut up!

John enters with a tray of food, still wearing his guitar.

JOHN. Anne? Hey, hey, slow down. You been drinking? You need something to eat?
ANNE. John, what is this?
JOHN. It's this new thing I just found out about. It's called…a charcuterie board.
ANNE. No! I don't mean this! I mean, what is happening here?
JOHN. I wanted to see you.
ANNE. Oh really? And?
JOHN. I wanted you to meet Moh-nica. I thought you'd really like her.
ANNE. Excuse me?
JOHN. We met at one of my gigs. She does A&R. You know, scouting for bands. Can you believe it? But that's not why she's here-
ANNE. Why is she here?
JOHN. What is this? I thought we were cool.
ANNE. Cool?
JOHN. Yeah, aren't we? We're friends, right?
ANNE. What? You are blowing my mind right now. How did you think this would be ok?
JOHN. I thought you could handle it.
ANNE. Handle what?
JOHN. We broke up like a month ago.
ANNE. What?!
JOHN. Yeah, you know, we both got so busy and you were canceling dates-
ANNE. No, you were canceling dates, you were.
JOHN. Hey, you canceled a few, too.

ANNE. Yeah because I was mad at you. But, we just
        went to New York for Valentine's Day. We
        went to the 9/11 museum. It was so romantic.
JOHN. Yeah, it was. I still really care about you.
ANNE. Do you?
JOHN. Hey… It's hard to let go. I thought we were
        like, taking the Band-Aid off slowly, you
        know? That it would be easier on you.
ANNE. Easier on me? Right now, giving me a
        lobotomy would be easier on me. Ugh, my head
        hurts.
JOHN. Come here. I know this is hard, that's why
        we're taking it one step at a time, ok? Let's just
        see what happens. Davey boy's here.
ANNE. (*muffled*) Yeah, so? Is he here as a buffer so I
        wouldn't kill you?
JOHN. (*amused*) I love how you always keep your
        sense of humor.
ANNE. Humor…the laughing, it stopped.
JOHN. What stopped?
ANNE. Something's changed, what is it?
JOHN. Why are you so adorable?
ANNE. Stop. You're making this so difficult.
JOHN. You're making this so difficult.

*They share a moment and lean in to kiss. David
enters and moves to push them apart.*

DAVID. Hey, hey, wowzers, am I right? What's, uh,
        happening over here?
JOHN. Nothing man, just talking with my Annie
        Bananie.

*John gives Anne's nose a tap. He gestures to
David to "go for it" and exits.*

DAVID. What are you doing?
ANNE. (*giddy*) He still loves me.
DAVID. No.
ANNE. What do you mean, "no"?
DAVID. He's just…being John. Don't fall for his
     bullshit, Anne. You deserve better than that.
ANNE. (*suspicious*) Did he ask you to be here tonight
     to talk me down, or something?
DAVID. No. No. That's not-
ANNE. No? Ok, then why? What are you doing here
     tonight? It was supposed to be just me and him.
     Why are you here?
DAVID. Ok, ok. (*Pause.*) John said you two were
     having some trouble. And, I don't know, we
     were talking about you, and I told him how
     great you are and how much fun we have when
     we see each other…and, he just asked me if I
     liked you.
ANNE. What are you saying, David?

David moves in to kiss Anne.

ANNE. No.

Laugh track.

ANNE. No!
DAVID. No?

*Laugh track sounds continuously, getting
louder and louder. Monica and John reenter.*

ANNE. No, I don't mean "no", I just…oh my head is
       spinning. Stop! I can't take this anymore!
MONICA. Are you ok, Anne?
DAVID. Anne? What's wrong?
ANNE. No!

*Anne covers her ears and screams, pushing
past everyone and exiting out the front door.
Full lights down, nighttime blue lights up. Anne
falls to the ground in a ball with her hands still
over her ears, sobbing. Luke, thirties, is
standing there with a scooter.*

LUKE. Uh, hey there.

Anne looks up.

LUKE. You ok there, cookie?
ANNE. No!
LUKE. Ok, no problem…you want to talk about it?
ANNE. No!

Anne wails some more.

LUKE. Oh hey, hey. It's ok. Whatever it is, let it out,
       babe.
ANNE. (*sobbing*) It's my boyfriend. And his best
       friend. And MOH-nica.
LUKE. Uh-oh, Moh-nica?
ANNE. I know.
LUKE. She sounds like the worst one of them all.
ANNE. But she's not, actually. I think if she wasn't
       dating my boyfriend, I'd really like her.
LUKE. Ok, that's interesting.

ANNE. Um, thank you…for being so kind.
LUKE. Hey, my mom always said a man should help a
        woman in need.
ANNE. Shouldn't everyone help anyone in need?
LUKE. Fair point. She is a bit old-fashioned. And I
        think my brother took that to mean he should
        date every woman in need, so…
ANNE. Oh my god. You're Luke, John's twin brother.
LUKE. That's me.
ANNE. Wow. You two look nothing alike.
LUKE. Oh, fraternal twins. Yeah, he always forgets to
        tell people that.
ANNE. Well it's nice to finally meet you.
LUKE. You too, Anne. (*Pause.*) I'm sorry about your
        birthday.
ANNE. Oh. Thank you.
LUKE. Yeah when John told me it was your birthday
        over my last visit, I was so mad at him. He can
        be such a douche.
ANNE. I think he was just excited to see you.
LUKE. You don't have to stand up for him.
ANNE. I know.
LUKE. So now that I understand some of this, uh,
        situation that brought you out here screaming,
        is there anything else I should know?
ANNE. Well, while John was introducing me to his
        new girlfriend, I think he was trying to set me
        up with his best friend.
LUKE. To Davey boy?
ANNE. Yeah.
LUKE. He's a great guy. But that's messed up.
ANNE. Yeah.
LUKE. Ok, I think I got the gist. Anything else?
ANNE. Well…I'm not sure you'll believe me.

LUKE. Try me.

ANNE. It just doesn't feel real. It's like everyone is an extreme version of themselves. And when the simplest, most stupid thing happens, I hear this…sound.

LUKE. Laughter.

ANNE. Oh my god, yes! But it's not coming from anyone in the room. It's like a…a-

LUKE. Laugh track?

ANNE. Yes! A laugh track! I keep hearing this goddamn laugh track.

LUKE. Like you're in a sitcom.

ANNE. Yes! How did you know?

LUKE. This is what always happens for the most important moments in life! Like when something amazing you never thought would happen to you actually does, the universe drops you right into the most incredible movie you've ever seen and you're living out a dream come true. But other times, when misfortune hits, it sticks you into a bad sitcom where everyone is laughing at you and the hits just keep coming and coming, and you try to bail out-

ANNE. I think that's what I just did.

LUKE. This won't end it, though. The silence won't last. The laugh track will find you again.

ANNE. So, what do I do now?

LUKE. You have to go back in there.

ANNE. Why?

LUKE. To finish what you started.

ANNE. I didn't even start this, he did!

LUKE. This is your story, Anne. You're the protagonist. What are you trying to do here tonight?

ANNE. I'm trying to make John love me again.
LUKE. Is it working?
ANNE. Yes! Well, it's confusing, he can be such a-
LUKE. Yes he can. And are you willing to put your life on hold for a guy like John?
ANNE. (*Pause.*) What is this, now? Is this like, *It's A Wonderful Life*? Are you my Clarence? Are you trying to get your wings? Do I have to make a bell ring, or…?
LUKE. What do you want, Anne?
ANNE. I just want answers.
LUKE. Okay. So you know what you came here to do.
ANNE. Yes, I do. I'm here to save the Building and Loan!
LUKE. Ok, enough with the *It's A Wonderful Life* references.
ANNE. Fine. But if I go back in there, it better be something cooler than this nightmare sitcom.
LUKE. Hm. Ok cookie, your wish is my command.

Luke snaps his fingers and the lights go out.

ANNE. Whoa, what the-? What is happening? Where did the moon go? Is this a lunar eclipse, or something? Hello? This is so weird. Hello?

Blue lights suddenly come back up. Luke is gone.

ANNE. Well that was crazy- Wait, Luke? Luke?! (*Pause.*) Clarence?

Laugh track.

ANNE. No, no, no! We are not starting that again!

> *Anne bursts through the doorway as lights
> come up on the apartment, moody, with deep
> shadows. Noir-style music plays. John is
> leaning against the cabinet smoking a cigar.
> Monica sits stunningly at the dining room table
> and David stands nearby, wearing suspenders
> and a fedora. They're all dressed in black and
> white, frozen in time.*

ANNE. Now this is more like it. All right you mooks,
    I'm back!

> *Monica, John and David unfreeze.*

MONICA. Anne! You're alive.
JOHN. See, I told you she wasn't dead.
DAVID. Interesting. Have a seat, Anne.

> *David grabs a chair and sets it in the center of
> the room. Anne sits.*

MONICA. Anne, we were so worried about you. You
    must be exhausted.
ANNE. Why would I be exhausted?
MONICA. Because of everything you've been
    through. Finding me here with John must have
    been quite a shock. And the way you ran out of
    here screaming, why, I thought you might do
    something horrible to yourself.
DAVID. Yes, quite the ordeal. Tell me, Anne, what
    was it that sent you flying out of here, without

so much as a backward glance? Was it them, or
        was it me?
ANNE. Heh, if you only knew.
DAVID. You led me to believe we were friends,
        maybe more than friends.
ANNE. What? You think I led you-
MONICA. Why else would you come here tonight?
ANNE. First of all, I had no idea about you, Moh-nica-
DAVID. It appears there were signs, Anne. You just
        didn't want to see them.
ANNE. Signs?
DAVID. Indeed. Like those large advertisements
        they're putting up all over town. Signs as big as
        buildings!
JOHN. I think they're called "billboards" Davey.
DAVID. Keep flapping your lips, Johnny! I've got
        questions for you next.
JOHN. Get a load of this guy, Annie.
ANNE. Don't play nice with me, John. This is all your
        fault.
MONICA. Seems Anne will lay the blame on everyone
        but herself.
ANNE. The blame for what? Why is everyone putting
        this on me? First Luke, now you two?
DAVID. Luke?
JOHN. When did you meet Luke?
MONICA. Who's Luke?
ANNE. Luke is John's twin brother. I never met him,
        until tonight.
JOHN. But how?
ANNE. He's in town, apparently. Why didn't you tell
        me you two are fraternal twins?
MONICA. What does that mean?
DAVID. It means they're not identical.

MONICA. So?

ANNE. So? John has been hiding his brother's true identity! Am I the only one who sees what's going on here? It's plain as day! John is the evil twin!

Lights out with spotlight on John, evil theme music plays as he laughs maniacally. Lights come back up and John returns to normal.

DAVID. No, no, no. He's not evil.

JOHN. I'm not?

ANNE. Yes he is!

DAVID. No. Anne, I've known Luke for years. His identity? Not a secret.

ANNE. But…but that's what Luke was trying to tell me. He was saying that he's the nice twin and John is the jerk.

JOHN. Hey!

DAVID. So "evil" is fine, but "jerk" is where you cross the line?

ANNE. I know he doesn't mean to be evil, or a jerk. He's just scared. John, you're using Moh-nica and David to push me away because…you're still in love with me.

JOHN. I told you, we broke up like a month ago, sweetheart.

ANNE. What? Do you hear yourself? What is going on in that head of yours? You know what? This isn't working, I'm outta here.

MONICA. Not so fast, Anne.

Monica pulls a gun and aims it at Anne.

JOHN. Moh-nica?

MONICA. You fools! My name isn't Moh-nica, how awful would that be? My name is…MAH-nica.

Lights out with spotlight on Monica who poses with the gun as dramatic music plays. Lights back up and she returns to normal.

JOHN. Is this a joke? Are you pulling my leg?

MONICA. I'm pulling more than that, John.

DAVID. Ok, no need to get vulgar.

MONICA. I'm pulling the strings, David, of this hatchet job of an evening. But it's all been for nothing, a bust. I was trying to get through to you, Anne. I thought we could both teach John a lesson.

ANNE. Then why are you pointing the gun at me?

MONICA. Sit, Anne. Sit, and listen. Maybe you'll learn something.

JOHN. Annie.

MONICA. Quiet, John.

Monica points the gun at John.

MONICA. Little Johnny boy. Playing us against each other. Telling poor Anne one thing and me another. You are a piece of work.

ANNE. Moh-nica, Mah-nica, I think you need to put the gun down now.

MONICA. But we have him right where we want him, Anne. He doesn't love me. You know what he loves?

ANNE. Me?

MONICA. No.

ANNE. You?
MONICA. No.
ANNE. David?
MONICA. No! His guitar!

They all nod.

MONICA. And suffering. He loves suffering under the
     burden of his own inadequacy, so he makes
     everyone around him suffer, too. I was never
     going to sign your band, John. I just wanted to
     see how far you'd take this ruse of a romance.
     As soon as Anne walked in, why, I knew it was
     over. Now, I'm going to teach you a lesson…
     and Anne is going to help me do it.

*Monica puts the gun in Anne's hands and she
and David help Anne aim it at John.*

ANNE. I really don't want-
MONICA. You know what you need to do. It's time to
     meet your maker, Johnny boy!

*Blackout and a gunshot is heard. Anne
screams.*

ANNE. No! John? John! Hello? Is anyone here? Oh,
     not again! This is so weird. Please turn the
     lights back on! Please turn the lights back on,
     now!

*The lights come up. It's only Anne and Luke,
Luke standing where John was. He's grabbing
his stomach like he's been shot.*

LUKE. Ya shot me, sweetheart!

*He moves to the chair Anne was in and
collapses, coughing periodically.*

LUKE. Hold me closer, Anne, it's getting dark!
ANNE. No!
LUKE. Tell Dorothy we're not in Kansas anymore.
ANNE. No!
LUKE. Houston, we have a problem.
ANNE. No!
LUKE. Luke, I am your father!

He passes out.

ANNE. No! No, Luke. Luke? Luke!
LUKE. (*hoarsely*) Try CPR.

*Luke purses his lips as though for Anne to kiss
him. She pushes him away.*

ANNE. Ugh, you're fine.
LUKE. Nice twist, cookie!
ANNE. Stop calling me that.
LUKE. Ok.
ANNE. What just happened? That got way out of
        hand. And this…this still can't be over.
LUKE. Obviously. That wasn't real life. You stopped
        the laugh track, but you didn't stop the show.
ANNE. What do you want from me?
LUKE. Stop acting like a victim, Anne. You are in
        charge of your own destiny. Free will, baby.
        You have a decision to make. So make it.
ANNE. What decision?

LUKE. You get one more try. (*Singing*) Clap on, clap
    off, the Clapper.

Luke claps twice and the lights go out.

ANNE. Are you kidding me? What is this? A
    decision? I have to make a decision. Fine, I
    make a decision, ok? Turn the lights back on!
    Turn the lights back on, now!

*David claps twice, the lights come back up. He
is dressed in modern clothes and lighting is
normal.*

DAVID. Listen, Anne, about what happened earlier…
    I'm sorry. I shouldn't have put you in that
    position, knowing how you feel about John.
ANNE. David, you were just being honest. But I'm not
    there, where you are.
DAVID. I understand.
ANNE. Still friends?
DAVID. Still friends.

*A pause, then David moves in to kiss her like
before.*

ANNE. No!
DAVID. Never mind.

*David moves downstage right as Monica
enters, also dressed modernly. Special on
David and special on Anne and Monica.*

MONICA. Hi Anne.

ANNE. Hey, Moh-ica? Or Mah-nica…which is it?
MONICA. Who gives a shit? Listen, I'm getting the
          feeling that things aren't over between you and
          John. He didn't really tell me how it ended with
          you two.
ANNE. He didn't really tell me either.
MONICA. Damn.
ANNE. Yeah. Do you think you can give John and I
          some privacy to…figure this out?
MONICA. My thoughts exactly. And don't worry,
          he'll get what's coming to him, they always do.

          They stand looking at each other for a moment,
          then Monica moves in to kiss Anne.

ANNE. No!
MONICA. Just kidding!

          Monica moves to downstage left special. John
          enters, dressed modernly.

ANNE. John.
JOHN. Annie.
ANNE. Don't, don't "Annie" me, John. You broke my
          heart. And I don't deserve this. If you're not in
          love with me anymore, you should just say so.
          (*Pause.*) And you can't just keep me around to
          turn me into David's girlfriend, either. That's
          not your decision. And it's definitely not what I
          want.
JOHN. What do you want?
ANNE. I want you to be different.
JOHN. I know. I'm not very good at this, I guess.
          Relationships.

ANNE. You're not a bad guy, John, you just need to use your powers for good.

Downstage specials go down on David and Monica, special remains on Anne and John.

JOHN. Maybe you're right. But hey, maybe the timing was bad. We might see each other again one day. Like, what if in ten years, if neither of us is married, we meet at the top of the Empire State Building-?
ANNE. John, stop. No more movies. This is real life, and sometimes things just end.
JOHN. Then, what do we do now?
ANNE. We say goodbye, John.
JOHN. Goodbye, Anne.

They shake hands. Special goes down as Anne exits out the front door and nighttime blue lights come up. She breathes a sigh of relief and reflects for a moment. Then, a bell rings. Anne looks around in wonder.

ANNE. Attaboy, Luke.

End of Play.

FA

by Henry Todd

Overview
a 25-minute dark comedy
for 9 actors, 2 female and 7 male

Synopsis
Chief Inspector Kismet is taking drastic measures
within his department to fulfill the City's federally
mandated birth quotas (or face nuclear obliteration),
but Director of the State Sanctioned Sexual Encounters
Agency, Gilchristendomshard, is at odds with Kismet's
directives.

Characters
KISMET   – male, 30s-50s
JESSUM   – male, 30s-40s
GILCHRISTENDOMSHARD – male, 30s-40s
MRS. RODRIGUEZ-MCCARTHY – female, 30s-40s
RECEPTIONIST   – female, 20s-40s
OFFICER 1   – male, 20s-50s
OFFICER 2   – male, 20s-50s
OFFICER 3   – male, 20s-50s
OFFICER 4   – male, 20s-50s

Setting
The future 10-30 years from present, full-fledged
fascist society.

Props
3 handguns, 1 silenced pistol, 5 machine guns, desk/chair, presidential photo, case files.

Original Premiere
Fa premiered on May 31st, 2025, at the 2025 Playhouse West Extravaganza One Act Fest, directed by Wolfgang Bodison.

Original Cast
KISMET — Sonny Schnapf
JESSUM — John O'Brien
GILCHRISTENDOMSHARD — Henry Todd
MRS. RODRIGUEZ-MCCARTHY — Melissa V. Rodriguez
RECEPTIONIST — Khyla Horton
OFFICER 1 — Patrick Kevin
OFFICER 2 — Kyle Tran
OFFICER 3 — Camilo Eraso
OFFICER 4 — Henry Foster Brown

Performance Rights
This play may not be performed, reproduced, or adapted without written permission from the author. To request performance rights, please contact Henry Todd, henryjamestodd@gmail.com, www.maretodd.com.

Scene 1

Kismet sits a desk with computer monitor, communications intercom and lamp. A photo of the President above him.

KISMET. Yes, Mr. McCarthy? This is Officer Kismet with the Secret Police. I stopped by about a week ago and had your house raided? *(response)* You remember! Good. And in addition to our little chat about finding terrorists (of which we found none, so good on you), you probably remember our other little chat about the plummeting birthrates? *(response)* Uh-huh, and how your household has no kids. And how that's… *(response)* Right. Illegal. One child per household at least. Right. *(response)* Then the courts ordered you had six days to get your wife, Mrs. Rodriguez-McCarthy, pregnant? *(beat)* You remember! Good. I have to narrow it to three days. *(response)* I don't care what the courts mandated I'm telling you that you have three days until I deploy the Sex Police! *(response)* I understand that it's... That word. Been a long time since I've heard that word... It doesn't matter whether or not it is that word. It is what it is. *(response)* No I head the Secret Police. You know: summary executions, kidnappings, torture; extraordinary rendition if the budget allows. The Sex Police are their own department. *(response)* You'd have to talk to Director Gilchristendomshard. Director Gil.christendom-shard. And Mr. McCarthy, watch your fucking mouth. That's a terrible word.

Kismet hangs up. Jessum barges in

JESSUM. The birthrates are plummeting, Kismet!

KISMET. *(annoyed)* Yeah, I know! I know they're plummeting! I just got off the phone cause they're plummeting!
That's all anybody can talk about these days- the fucking plummeting, plummeting, plummeting. And knock before coming in!

Kismet stands up, paces, looks out his window dramatically.

KISMET. This City's fucked, Jessum. The Mayor's expanding our budgets again but I don't think it's going to cut it. We're in trouble. The City isn't going to meet the federally mandated birth quotas. Fuck!

JESSUM. *(scoffs)* Where have all the men gone? Nothing but a bunch of soft pricks out there nowadays-

KISMET. It's the food! It's the water, Jessum! Damn it, the air! Bad particulate matter in the air! We've reaped what we've sown! Inform yourself!

JESSUM. Jeez, okay, I wasn't saying you had a soft (prick)-

KISMET. And don't forget the women! *(with distaste)* The women. Where are they? I don't see any women! I certainly don't see any women getting pregnant!

JESSUM. So, it's the women's fault!

KISMET. *(scoffs)* They share at least half the blame! Collapsing uteri! I mean, if we're going to be blamed for our soft pricks, then the women shall certainly be blamed for their collapsing uteri! The point is, Jessum, we're in fucking trouble!

JESSUM. We're not going to meet the City's birthrate quotas!!!

KISMET. *(beat)* No... Not unless we do something drastic.

Officer Gilchristendomshard knocks, comes in with a stack of organized files, each to a folder.

GILCHRISTENDOMSHARD. I just got a call from Mr. McCarthy and now I have some concerns about these case files, Officer Kismet.

KISMET. Oh. So formal, Director Gilchristendomshard, so formal. Thanks for knocking. But you see, I don't give a fuck that you have some concerns about those case files. And Mr. McCarthy is nothing but a poor-sported limp-dick loser. What are you- his friend? You know hi m?

GILCHRISTENDOMSHARD. Don't be ridiculous. We've got some serious business to address here.

KISMET. Oh! The Director of the Sex Police has serious business to bring to my attention! You have problems with the case files? Well, I have problems with the City! I've got the mayor on my ass! The birthrates are plummeting!

GILCHRISTENDOMSHARD. All anyone can talk
about are the birthrates.
KISMET. What the fuck do you think you exist for?
JESSUM. But that's what you said, Kismet! "The
Plummeting, plummeting, plummeting." Like a
mad man!
KISMET. Jessum.
GILCHRISTENDOMSHARD. It's not about the
birthrates.
KISMET. Oh?
JESSUM. Ha! Not about the birthrates!? Of course it's
about the birthrates!
KISMET. Jessum.
GILCHRISTENDOMSHARD. Not at all. It's about
modes of desire. Motivational salience.
KISMET. Right. Uh. Sure. Of course! Because. The
President is... At war with motivational
salience?
GILCHRISTENDOMSHARD. You say that like a
question; you should know. If you're a true fa-
scist.
KISMET. I'm as fascist as clarified butter.
GILCHRISTENDOMSHARD. Then prove it.
KISMET. Prove it?! This is insubordination! I'll have
you killed! Jessum!

Jessum starts to move in on him.

GILCHRISTENDOMSHARD. I report to the Mayor,
not to you, Kismet! Only he can have me
killed.

*Jessum stops, looks at Kismet. Kismet tries to
remember.*

KISMET. Well. Fuck you Gilchristendomshard.

GILCHRISTENDOMSHARD. No, fuck you, because the courts mandated the date May sixteenth in the filing with- Mrs. Christina Rodriguez Mc-Carthy, for example- Yet I see May 13th for the execution date in the case file.

KISMET. I see. You. Read the court filings and not just the case files?

GILCHRISTENDOMSHARD. Of course. I'm Director of the State Sanctioned Sexual Encounters Agency; I take this position very seriously.

KISMET. So fucking young and righteous! Look at him! Won't- won't- won't… Rape the missus' until the date the court orders!

GILCHRISTENDOMSHARD. I'm simply following the law. And did you say... Rape? A bit of an superannuated word, don't think you think, Of-ficer Kismet?

KISMET. Oh, don't get semantical with me. Don't spit out your fancy words and abstractions again! Let's just call it what it is!

GILCHRISTENDOMSHARD. It's the State Sanc-tioned Sexual Encounters Agency, Kismet! Not the sex police. Certainly not the. Well. Other word Police.

KISMET. We've got to take drastic measures! The courts say one thing. The mayor says another thing. I say something quite like a perfect cohe-sion between the fucking two. Who enforces the courts?!

GILCHRISTENDOMSHARD. We do.

KISMET. Exactly- we... Do.

GILCHRISTENDOMSHARD. So, I'll be doing just that.

KISMET. You follow my directive, Officer Gilchristendomshard, or I'll… Send Jessum to carry out
  those executions.
JESSUM. Jeez. You think we could get some of the
  guys to help? Those look like a lot of files.
KISMET. We're spread too thin, Jessum.
JESSUM. I can't rape twenty women in one day!
GILCHRISTENDOMSHARD. Listen to your subordinates, Kismet.
KISMET. You say subordinates as if there are more
  than one. Take a look. Nobody is here! Just this
  idiot! All the rest are manning the fucking thou-
  sand security checkpoints across the City!
GILCHRISTENDOMSHARD. Then I guess you'll just
  have to follow the court's directive.
KISMET. Listen to me, Gilchristendomshard! This is
  bigger than you, me, the mayor and the fucking
  courts! It's the Fed, you understand? The President has threatened nuclear obliteration for any
  city that doesn't meet the birth quota!

A beat, then Gilchristendomshard laughs.

GILCHRISTENDOMSHARD. We're at war with
  modes of desire and motivational salience and
  you're worried about nuclear obliteration?
KISMET. I. Wait. What?
GILCHRISTENDOMSHARD. I watch the news,
  Kismet, I'm well aware. The Mayor said the
  same thing. You want to talk about nuclear
  obliteration? That's just bad policy. We're talking about the inner sanctum of human slippage.
KISMET. Look, I may not be into all that new-age fascist semantical crap you young people are

spouting these days, but I came up as a true thug. A real rough-shirt. I broke laws I didn't like. I broke faces I didn't like. If there's anything a good fascist knows is that the law applies to some, not to others, and only sometimes, depending on expediency, power. Cruelty. Don't forget cruelty, young man. Cruelty is the point.

GILCHRISTENDOMSHARD. *(hesitates)* Well, of course! As any good fascist knows... Glad we could clear this up.

KISMET. No, no, we're not done here!

GILCHRISTENDOMSHARD. We are. I uphold the court's order. The wives have 6 days before the State Sanctioned Sexual Encounters Agents are deployed. And, who knows, they might very well get impregnated by their respective husbands in the meanwhile. Which is really the outcome we want, isn't it Kismet? Isn't that the point of all this?

KISMET. Yeah, sure.

Gilchristendomshard begins to exit, stops at the door.

GILCHRISTENDOMSHARD. And for the morale of my men perhaps we could refrain from calling it...

KISMET. What? Calling it what? Say it!

GILCHRISTENDOMSHARD. They get tired of it. They're already called- that- so often out in the field. My boys deserve a break.

JESSUM. I understand, Officer Gilchristendomshard. I need a break.

KISMET. *(can't believe it)* Jessum, what are you...
     (doing?)
JESSUM. I may not be in the Sex Police, but I am a
     rapist.
KISMET. Jessum! Not now! The Department's thera-
     pist is literally down the hall! Go! Now!
JESSUM. I already told you I don't need a therapist!
     I've figured it out without a therapist. I am a
     rapist.
KISMET. Goodness fucking gracious.
JESSUM. And that is why I would never carry out
     your orders, Kismet!

Kismet hesitates.

KISMET. But that doesn't... (make any sense.)
JESSUM. Just because I am a rapist, doesn't mean I
     have to rape anybody! There's an odd moment
     between all three. All are a bit confused.
     Gilchristendomshard laughs.
GILCHRISTENDOMSHARD. You're an honorable
     man, Officer Jessum. But you won't have to
     worry about that.
KISMET. *(to Jessum)* Uh. No. You will have to worry
     about that- *(to Gilchristendomshard)* Because
     you are going to do what the fuck I say!
GILCHRISTENDOMSHARD. That so?
KISMET. Oh yeah!
GILCHRISTENDOMSHARD. How do you intend to
     enforce your order?

Tense pause between the two. Gilchristen-
domshard smoothly draws his pistol while
Kismet fumbles for his.

Jessum, after a moment, draws his gun and points it at Gilchristendomshard. Kismet is encouraged.

KISMET. Yes, exactly! Good! You see? My man here will enforce my order-

JESSUM. I'll enforce your stupid minusthree- day-order or whatever! But I'm not going to be the one to carry it out!

KISMET. Don't worry, Jessum! The Sex Police will do it!

GILCHRISTENDOMSHARD. If you shoot me you'll be left with 179 case files. And that's just this week alone.

JESSUM. My goodness fuck! 179 case files!? Get McClevenson to do it! Anyone! Anyone but me! You do it!

KISMET. McClevenson has erectile dysfunction! Okay?! They all have erectile dysfunction! *(beat, embarrassed)* I. I have erectile dysfunction.

JESSUM. I'm sorry, boss.

KISMET. You think Gilchristendomshard or any of that department have that problem!? Of course not! They've been screened and tested and they all have very uh- goodfunctioning. We have no choice!

GILCHRISTENDOMSHARD. Oh, I hardly go out in the field anymore.

KISMET. *(impassioned)* Shut up, rapist!

GILCHRISTENDOMSHARD. *(beat)* I'm doing my job, Kismet. Just like you.

KISMET. *(leans in, impassioned)* Well then do your fucking job! Do it three days prior to the date the stupid courts ordered or my man, Jessum here, will shoot you. Haha!

GILCHRISTENDOMSHARD. *(to Jessum)* Officer Jessum, if you shoot me on his order you both will be tried for crimes against civility! And we all know the punishment for crimes against civility.

Jessum and Kismet look at each other.

GILCHRISTENDOMSHARD. That's right. A certain surgical amendment. *(beat)* You wouldn't have to worry about your erectile dysfunction anymore, Kismet.

Gilchristendomshard laughs and holsters his gun.

GILCHRISTENDOMSHARD. This is ridiculous. Bottomline, we will execute when our Agency sees fit to execute.

KISMET. Listen, stop being crazy for like two seconds! If you deploy three days earlier we can make the birth quotas! It's only three days!

GILCHRISTENDOMSHARD. Exactly. Only three days. Why are we fighting?

KISMET. Yet you're so determined.

GILCHRISTENDOMSHARD. Gentlemen.

He exits and Kismet calls after him.

KISMET. You're compromised, Gilchristendomshard!

A beat. Gilchristendomshard comes back. He laughs.

GILCHRISTENDOMSHARD. Compromised?
KISMET. *(beat)* Which one of them are you fucking?

For the first time Gilchristendomshard looks visibly shaken. He scoffs.

GILCHRISTENDOMSHARD. What?
KISMET. Mrs. Rodriguez McCarthy. You know how I know that? Cause I know these case files as good as you do. And so, I know Mrs. Rodriguez-McCarthy as much as I know Mrs. Williams. *(beat)* Mr. Williams and Mrs. Williams, they don't have a sex problem; it just so happens Mr. Williams fires blanks. Nothing they can do about it, quite tragic. Williams has average erection sizes according to our data. But Mrs. Rodriguez- McCarthy? Oh yes, she has a sex problem. And in case you don't know what I mean, I'm saying Mr. McCarthy has erectile dysfunction! *(beat)* Seems like she's solved her problem, however.

Gilchristendomshard is left silent. Jessum realizes Kismet is right and is wowed and basks in his Boss's glory.

JESSUM. Oh shit!!! Mark one win for Kismet, finally!
KISMET. Jessum. *(to Gilchristendomshard)* So here's what's going to happen, Officer Gilchristendomshard. If you don't carry out these executions early- including Mrs. Rodriguez- Mc-

Carthy's... I'll go to the Mayor with what I know. What was it you said about crimes against civility again? Certain surgical amendments? Uh-oh. No more erections for you, I guess.

Kismet has been walking closer during this short monologue. He steps close to Gilchristendomshard.

KISMET. What were the dates on those case files again? Was it May 16th?
GILCHRISTENDOMSHARD. *(beat)* Of course not. May 13th.
KISMET. Oh, okay. Just checking. Bam!!!

Kismet and Jessum celebrate, run victory laps. Then a receptionist enters.

RECEPTIONIST. Mr. Kismet.
KISMET. Yes, Sweet Cheeks?
RECEPTIONIST. Somebody is here to file a report of pregnancy with your office but she's requesting the presence of Director Gilchristendomshard.
KISMET. *(annoyed)* Yeah, tell her he operates his own department that do their own things, okay? Mainly rape. Point is, I'm the guy she wants to talk to if she has any fucking caveats! And I will not be talking to Mrs. Rodriguez-Mc-Carthy right now!
GILCHRISTENDOMSHARD. Bring her in, Ms. Rose.
RECEPTIONIST. Yes, Director.

*The receptionist smiles at Gilchristendomshard
and exits.*

KISMET. What? No! I'm not taking any fucking ap-
	pointments right now. Sweet cheeks- I mean,
	Ms. Rosecome back here!

Mrs. Rodriguez-McCarthy enters. Long silence.

JESSUM. *(in awe)* Oh my God.
KISMET. Missus Rodriguez-McCarthy.
GILCHRISTENDOMSHARD. Christina.
CHRISTINA RODRIGUEZ-MCCARTHY. Hello
	Paul.
KISMET. Officer Gilchristendomshard, I'm glad we
	could clear all that up; you can leave my office
	now. Mrs. Rodriguez-McCarthy you have a re-
	port of pregnancy you'd like to bring to my at-
	tention I guess?
CHRISTINA RODRIGUEZ-MCCARTHY. Yes, I'm
	pregnant. I have the ultrasounds to prove it. I
	found out this morning.
GILCHRISTENDOMSHARD. Are you really?
CHRISTINA RODRIGUEZ-MCCARTHY. *(joyous)*
	Yes!

She sings to high heaven.

CHRISTINA RODRIGUEZ-MCCARTHY. Paul
	Gilchristendomshard is the father!

*Kismet sees the moment between them and is
absolutely disgusted.*

KISMET. Okay I don't know what this is but both of
      you get the hell out of my office before I arrest
      you-
GILCHRISTENDOMSHARD. You know what this
      means, Kismet?

Kismet hesitates.

KISMET. Uhm. Nothing at all. I still have you by the
      balls. You committed adultery. Crime of civil-
      ity! Off with your penis!
GILCHRISTENDOMSHARD. Not at all. I'm the fa-
      ther. I clearly impregnated her while in the
      field. It's a state-sanctioned progeny.
KISMET. Uh! No! Cause the execution wasn't carried
      out until May 13th. And today is May 10th!
CHRISTINA RODRIGUEZ-MCCARTHY. I'll just
      file it later then!

*Gilchristendomshard and she smile at each
other.*

KISMET. No, you'll file it now!
JESSUM. Boss! You're just being spiteful! Let her file
      it in three days.
KISMET. Jessum! I told you we needed to take drastic
      measures.
JESSUM. So they'll do the executions on the sixteenth
      instead of the thirteenth! Who cares! A Hun-
      dred seventy nine rapes a week seems like
      enough to me!
KISMET. It's not enough! Birth quotas! Nuclear oblit-
      eration! Deregulation causes collapsing uteri

and soft penises. The plummeting, plummeting, plummeting! I'm just doing my fucking job!
GILCHRISTENDOMSHARD. And I'm doing mine.

Gilchristendomshard and Christina begin to exit.

JESSUM. Damn it… *(beat)* Christina!

Christina stops, turns around, somewhat surprised.

JESSUM. Please. If you will have me. Let me be the one to impregnate you next.
KISMET. Jessum!

Gilchristendomshard laughs.

GILCHRISTENDOMSHARD. Let's go Christina.

He starts to go but sees that Christina hasn't moved yet, still looking at Jessum, he at her. Kismet is revulsed.

KISMET. This is unbelievable.
GILCHRISTENDOMSHARD. Christina.
CHRISTINA RODRIGUEZ-MCCARTHY. Coming, Paul.

One final look and then she turns around and walks out with Paul G.

KISMET. Trust me: Don't get mixed up with Mrs. Rodriguez-McCarthy.

JESSUM. Why not?

KISMET. Because! She's bad news. Obviously! I
       mean, she boinked the Director of the Sex Po-
       lice behind her husband's back! Now she's
       having his baby!

JESSUM. Her husband sounds like... What was it you
       said? A poor-sported, limpdick loser?

KISMET. That's insensitive- he has erectile
       dysfunction. Mrs. Rodriguez- McCarthy is hun-
       gry, okay? I'm warning you.

JESSUM. I'm happy to hear she's hungry. I would
       gladly feed her.

KISMET. Jessum, she uses sex strictly as a weapon!

JESSUM. What do you expect from females in a male-
       dominated world? I would gladly get lost in her
       vagina.

KISMET. Jessum, that's treasonous and stupid, watch
       your fucking mouth!

JESSUM. I hope she takes me.

KISMET. I'm sure she will.

*Three police-looking individuals enter. Two of
them raid the place.*

KISMET. What the hell is this?

OFFICER 1. Chief Inspector Kismet?

KISMET. Yeah, what?!

OFFICER 1. Officer Jessum?

KISMET. You've got the wrong guys actually.

OFFICER 1. You're both being charged with crimes
       against civility.

*Kismet and Jessum look at each other, horri-
fied.*

KISMET. What the hell for!?

OFFICER 1. Chief Inspector Kismet, disobeying court orders.

KISMET. Oh, c'mon! Nobody actually listens to those fucking clerks in wigs!

OFFICER 1. Officer Jessum, lewd displays of affection.

JESSUM. Lewd displays of affection?

OFFICER 1. Where's Director of the State Sanctioned Sexual Encounters Agency, Gilchristendomshard?

KISMET. Wait, he's being charged too?

OFFICER 1. Yes, of course. He committed unsanctioned sexual acts using his official title.

KISMET. Booya! Rule of law!

OFFICER 1. Where's Missus Rodriguez-McCarthy?

JESSUM. No, she's being charged too?

OFFICER 1. Of course.

Odd beat.

KISMET. Not for unsanctioned sexual acts using her official title?

OFFICER 1 She has no official title other than Missus. *(to Officer 2)* Haul them off.

Officer 1 motions for Officer 2 to cuff them, which they do.

JESSUM. Please don't! This is so embarrassing! Can you please just shoot us?

KISMET. Jessum!

OFFICER 1. The punishment must fit the crime, Officer Jessum. According to the Judge you don't deserve to die. Only be neutered.

As Kismet and Jessum are exited by Officer 2, Gilchristendomshard comes in, already cuffed, Officer 3 trying to restrain him.

GILCHRISTENDOMSHARD. Cadet! Who the hell do you think you are enforcing laws when you see fit!
OFFICER 1. Orders come from the Mayor. *(beat, looks at G)* The numbers aren't what they should be, Director. Your "sex police" are performing at suboptimal rates.
GILCHRISTENDOMSHARD. And how would a cadet like you know something like that?
OFFICER 1. I'm no cadet. I'm your replacement.

Officer 1 nods at Officer 3 who unholsters his gun and shoots Gilchristendomshard in the head. Moments later, Jessum, being restrained by Officer 2, pleads through the door frame.

JESSUM. That! I'll take that! Please! Shoot me, shoot me in the head!!
OFFICER 1. Restrain him!

Jessum fends Officer 2 off, even with hands cuffed. Officer 2 draws his gun. Jessum does kicks and whatever else he can do.

JESSUM. Ha! What are you going to do! Shoot me!? That's what I want!

Officer 2 shoots Jessum dead. Kismet comes in.

KISMET. I've decided I'd rather be shot.
OFFICER 1. Restrain him! He's getting neutered! It's
    the law!
KISMET. No I'm nooooot!

*Kismet (also cuffed) charges Officer 1 and Offi-
cer 2 shoots Kismet dead in response.*

OFFICER 3. Dude! That's a summary execution!
OFFICER 2. You're one to talk!

*Officer 4 comes in (hearing that) with Christina
restrained. (Officer 1 is waking up.)*

OFFICER 4. Summary execution!? You've killed the
    prisoners! You've gone rogue!

*Officer 4 unholsters his gun and Officer 2
shoots 4 & Christina.*

OFFICER 3. You did it again!
OFFICER 2. *(starts crying)* Stop criticizing ME!!!

*Officer 2 aims his gun at Officer 3 and shoots
him. Officer 1 looks around, processing what
happened.*

OFFICER 1. Holy shit! Everyone's dead!
OFFICER 2. I was protecting you, Director!
OFFICER 1. Oh my god this is a disaster. I've lost this
    promotion before I've even gotten it.

Officer 2 shoots himself. The phone rings and Officer 1 answers it.

OFFICER 1. Mr. Mayor? Yeah, all is- under control. I'll be getting those numbers up by the end of today, believe-you-me!

The Receptionist comes in and shoots Officer 1. Picks up the headpiece. Speaks.

RECEPTIONIST. Yes, Mr. Mayor? Yes, he completely botched the entire thing. I killed him. You're welcome. I told you: never send a fascist to do a woman's job.

The Receptionist laughs to no end. The whole place goes up in nuclear obliteration.

End of Play.